Happy Wife... Happy Life!

Dr. Benny Tate

ISBN 0-9706117-5-7

Design and Production
Riverstone Group, LLC, Canton, GA

Scripture quotations are from the King James Bible.

Printed in Canada

DEDICATION

This book is dedicated to a person who believes in me more than I believe in myself—Clayton Jones. The Bible says, "A friend loveth at all times . . ." (Proverbs 17:17); and Clayton Jones has been that friend to me. He has walked in when many others walked out and has been a constant support and encouragement to my life.

Thanks to Clayton for leading a young boy from the wrong side of the tracks to Christ many years ago and then always encouraging him to dream big and keep on keeping on. It is my honor to dedicate this book to you.

CONTENTS

FOREWORD

Dr. Benny Tate has pastored the same church for thirteen years, and he loves people. He has a kind, generous spirit; his heart is deeply rooted in the family. Married to the same woman for nearly nineteen years and raising their daughter, Benny has learned a great deal about the challenges, the difficulties, and the joys of keeping a family together and Christ-centered in this day and age.

In spite of the title, *Happy Wife, Happy Life*, this book is not just for husbands. Benny reaches out to every longing heart and family. In his unique, gifted style, he brings encouragement to the discouraged, hope to the hurting, and motivates the disheartened.

Sprinkled with humor, Benny brings the seriousness of God's Word to life and helps us understand what it really means for husbands to love their wives, for wives to respect their husbands, for children to obey their parents, and for each of us to be wholly submitted to God's will for our lives.

Thank you, Dr. Benny Tate, for obeying God's call and ministering to our families.

S. Truett Cathy
Founder & CEO, Chick-fil-A

ACKNOWLEDGEMENTS

To my wife Barbara for always being supportive of my call and ministry. Your don't play the piano or head up the Women's Missionary Society, but you have been the best pastor's wife anyone could have hoped for. Thanks for your encouragement and understanding during the writing of this book. I love you with all my heart.

To the greatest daughter in the world, Savannah Abigail. Savannah, I had rather be your dad than be president. Remember, we chose you; and if I had it to do all over, I would choose you a million times again. I am honored to be your dad.

To Tammy Cochran for your administrative assistance on this project. Thanks for typing, retyping, and proofing my manuscript. Anyone who can read my writing deserves to be honored in that alone. You went way above and beyond the call of duty. Thanks a million.

To my publisher Ernest Pullen and the Riverstone Group for being a calming force for an inexperienced writer.

To Rock Springs Church for allowing me to serve as the pastor for the greatest people on earth.

To my church board—Chairman Sam Perdichizzi, Don Faunce, Don Thomas, Robbie Kinard, Sam Pelt, Ray Bitrick, Neil Blalock, Phillip Cook, Bobby Cain, and Hank Boynton— for supporting the vision God has placed on my heart.

To the greatest staff anywhere: Stan, Steve, Cameron, Renee, Deb, and

Betty—you make coming to work fun.

To my mother Melba Williams for teaching me to never quit.

To my brothers and sisters—Terry, Mike, Kevin, Rhonda, Vicki, and Donna—for the joy you have brought to my life.

To Pastors Ralph Shrum and Wayne Gipson for taking a chance on me in the early days.

To Pastors Don Henley, Carl Cureton, Tommy Chapman, Jay Daughtery, David Watson, Bill Purvis, Steve Stewart, Mandel Nunley, Tim Conort, and Phillip Knight for being more than colleagues. You have been friends.

Last and most importantly, I owe everything I have and hope to be to Jesus Christ. Truly, I am just a sinner saved by grace; and God has given me the privilege to serve Him as a pastor. Yes, He has given me the honor to proclaim the Gospel of Christ; and I would never stoop down to be president. Thank You, Jesus, for life and life more abundantly.

CHAPTER ONE

A few years ago, a movie was released titled "What Women Want" starring Mel Gibson and Helen Hunt. I am not endorsing this movie because I did not see it. A review I read said it had sexual content and adult language, which I strongly disagree with; however, the plot was intriguing to me. In the movie, Mel Gibson had the uncanny ability to read women's minds and, in turn, was able to determine what they liked or disliked. Men, wouldn't this ability be great? But the truth of the matter is that we do not. Men, even though we do not have this ability, the Word of God teaches we are to meet the needs of our wives. With that being said, I am convinced there are six things every woman needs.

First, *every woman needs understanding.* The Bible says, "Likewise, ye husbands, dwell with them according to knowledge . . ." (1 Peter 3:7). We should become students of our wives.

I love the story about the man who was taking his morning walk on the beach when a bottle floated to shore and out popped a genie. She immediately told the man he could make one wish and – no matter what the circumstances – it would be granted. He shared how he had always wanted to go to

Honolulu, Hawaii, but was terrified to fly. Therefore, he requested a bridge be constructed from California to Hawaii. The genie thought intensely and then stated, "With the concrete and steel involved, the depth of the Pacific Ocean, and the logistics that would have to be considered, this would not be possible." Then she asked if he had a second request. He said, "Well, I have been married four times; and what I would really like is to understand women." The genie then asked, "Did you want two lanes or four on that bridge?"

It is interesting to me that God never told women to understand men, but He did tell men to understand women. God knows that for a man to properly lead his wife, he must understand her.

Here are four suggestions for men concerning understanding their wives:

1. Pray every day for understanding. (James 1:5)

2. Practice looking at things from her perspective. Instead of putting her "in her place," put yourself there.

3. When she is hurt, give her space and time. Women hurt at a much deeper level than men. My philosophy is admit it, quit it, and forget it. But when a woman has been hurt, it takes time for her to heal. Men, women are different from us!

4. Erase from your vocabulary: "You shouldn't feel that way."

Second, *every woman needs honor.* The Bible says, "Likewise, ye husbands, dwell with them according to knowledge, giving honour unto the wife . . ." (1 Peter 3:7). I have heard men say, "I would honour my wife if . . ." But "honour" in this text has nothing to do with performance; it has to do with position. It is assigning your wife a special rank or standing.

A strong-willed and opinionated lady passed away in a small rural town. This was before embalming. She left specific instructions for her funeral service. The day of the funeral, the pallbearers were carrying her casket across a small stream when one of the men stumbled and nearly fell. This sudden thrust apparently revived the lady, and she sat up in the casket. She lived ten more years after the incident. When she died "again," she had the exact same arrangements. This time as the pallbearers began to cross the stream, the husband stopped them and said, "Careful, boys!"

Men, honoring our wives is important. I am convinced that Dad sets the pace for how Mom is treated in the home. If we as fathers dishonor our wives, our children will also dishonor them more times than not.

Below are four ways to dishonor our wives.

1. Be critical of her in public.

2. Be critical of her in her absence.

3. Interrupt her when she is talking. When doing so, you are telling others as well as her that what you have to say is more important.

4. Allow your children to disrespect her and talk to her in the wrong tone of voice.

Third, *every woman needs love expressed.* The Bible teaches us to love our wives as Christ loved the church. (Ephesians 5:25) He expressed His love by dying on the cross at Calvary. Men should express love to their wives.

A wife was extremely depressed, and her husband became so concerned that he took her to the doctor himself. The doctor came in and assessed the woman's case. He then hugged her and kissed her right on the mouth. The sadness immediately left, and she was smiling from ear to ear. The doctor then looked at the bewildered husband and said, "Three times a week, brother!" The man stated, "I can bring her in on Mondays, Wednesdays, and Fridays."

This is a humorous story, but the truth is many men have difficulty expressing love to their wives. This is a vital need of every woman. Recent research gives several things women want from a sexual relationship:

1. They want to be close. More than 90 percent of women surveyed said they enjoy physical and emotional closeness best.

2. They want to spend time together. They want romantic dinners, evening walks, and vacations alone with their mate.

3. They want time for talking.

4. They want romance. When it comes to sex, men are like microwaves; they heat up fast. Women are like crock-pots; it takes time. Women are motivated by complimentary words, embracing, tenderness, and affection. They want romance.

5. They want to be able to say, "Not now." Most women would prefer a hug over a sexual experience. Men, learn to hug your wife without being Oscar the octopus!

6. They want to be appreciated for more than sex.

7. They want to please their husbands.

Fourth, *every woman needs appreciation expressed.* The Song of Solomon is a beautiful example of appreciation expressed. Over and over, Solomon is expressing his appreciation for his Shulamite Bride: "Thou hast ravished my heart . . ." (4:9). ". . . how much better is thy love than wine!" (4:10). ". . . O thou fairest among women" (6:1). Many men need to learn the power of words and how saying the right words are so important!

Mark Twain once said the difference between the right word and the nearly right word is the difference between lightning and a lightning bug. Let me give you an example: "When I look at you, time stands still." This will get you a hug. But "you have the face that could stop a clock" will get you hit! The right words of expression are vital!

Maybe this Dear Abby letter sums up what I am trying to say. It reads:

Dear Abby: I have been married for seventeen years. My husband never tells me I look pretty. I know some women reading your column will think, 'Who cares what somebody else thinks of you?' He tells my daughter she looks pretty – and the girls in his office, so I know he knows how to give a compliment.

Abby, I am not overweight. I wear makeup and get my hair cut every six weeks. I am not homely. I shower twice a day.

A year ago, I told my husband how I felt. Now the only time he says anything complimentary to me is when we are in bed. Too late! I need to hear encouraging words. Every woman needs to hear that she's attractive.

If you print this, maybe it will alert some nice husband out there who has been withholding to say, "Honey, you look pretty today." It'll sure go a long way with this wife. – **Desperate for a Compliment**

Fifth, **every woman needs security.** When the Bible says for the husband to be the head of the wife, God is not doing something to the wife; He is doing something for the wife. God, in His omniscience, knew a great need of every woman is security which comes mostly from the husband. This is why it is vitally important that the husband be the spiritual leader in the home. Husbands, she cannot follow a parked car. If you are not being the spiritual leader, you should be – START TODAY!

Dr. James Dobson says there are seven ways to build your wife's security:

1. Say "I love you" often.
2. Keep a job. (Many men are seeking employment but not work!)
3. Make long-range plans together.
4. Always be honest.
5. Be committed to Christ and His Church.
6. Value her thoughts and feelings.
7. Pray with her and for her.

Sixth, *every woman needs to be listened to.* A man asked his wife what she wanted for her birthday. She told him she would love to be ten again. With that being said, he woke her up early the next morning and took her to Six Flags. They rode the Scream Machine, the Mindbender, the Free-Fall, the Viper, the Batman . . . you name it – they rode it! Then they went to McDonald's for lunch; and he ordered both of them a Big Mac, fries, and a chocolate shake. After they ate, they went to the movies to see *102 Dalmatians.* Finally, after a full day of fun, they got home and the lady collapsed in bed. Her husband looked at her and asked, "What's it like being ten again?" She said, "I actually meant in dress size." Listening is a precious art.

From my experience as a pastor and counselor for more than twenty years, one word describes why women divorce their husbands: *neglect.* The problem shows itself in the words they say. Here are some examples.

1. "My husband is no longer my friend."
2. "The only time he pays any attention to me is when he wants sex."
3. "He is never there for me when I need him most."
4. "He lives his life as if we weren't married. He rarely considers me."
5. "I hurt all the time because I feel alone and abandoned."
6. "We're like ships passing in the night. He goes one way, and I go the other."
7. "My husband has become a stranger to me. I don't even know him anymore."
8. "He doesn't show any interest in me or what I do."

I serve as an evangelist, a denominational leader, a radio host, an author, and a pastor of the greatest group of people in the world. But my number-one responsibility is to meet the needs of my wife. No, she does not compete with my ministry; she is my first responsibility in ministry. I trust you will join me in attempting to meet the needs of the woman in your life.

C H A P T E R   T W O

The Bible is very clear that the husband is to be the leader of the home. Sadly, many times in our society that is not the case. I love the fictitious story about a group of men who arrived one day in Heaven. Peter asked those who were the leaders of their home to line up on the right and the ones who were not the leaders to line up on the left. Thirty-eight men lined up in the left line; and only one small, timid, frail man went to the right. Peter asked the man, "Why do you deserve to be in this line?" He answered, "This is the line my wife told me to get in."

During horse-and-buggy days, a young man was getting married. He shared with his father just how excited he was to become the leader of his home. He told his dad that once you are married and you are the man, you automatically become the leader. His father said, "Son, do you really believe that?" The son emphatically said, "Yes!" The father said, "Son, I want to teach you a valuable lesson. Go and hook up the wagon, load up the chickens, and go door to door throughout our town, asking husbands and wives together who is the leader of the home. If the husband is the head, give him a horse; but if the wife is the head, give her a chicken."

After the son visited nine homes, he had given away nine chickens. He arrived at the tenth home and asked the wife, "Who is the head of your home?" They both responded that it was the husband. The young man was greatly surprised but then explained that they would get to choose one of the two horses he had. The man looked at the horses and immediately chose the black one. His wife looked at him sternly and said, "I like the white one." He quickly responded, "We'll take the white horse." "No," the young man said, "you'll take a chicken."

A few years back, I received the following anonymous letter:

Pastor,
The man is the head of the home, but how will he know how to lead?
Does leadership come naturally at salvation or marriage? He loves Jesus
and his family. What if he thinks he's leading, but he doesn't really lead?
Instead the burden is on his wife to meet all the needs in the family, to
take care of the money, to set goals, to make the plans and decisions, to
cook, to comfort, to clean, and even to work too. There's no talking to
him about it. He just gets angry to hear that I have needs, to hear that
the burden is crushing Jesus and his family – and he thinks he's leading.

The lady is speaking for many women in our world today. I believe scores of women are crying out for a husband who is the leader God has called him to be.

Gary Smalley shared in his book *Winning Your Wife Back Before It Is Too Late* five qualities the women surveyed wanted in their husbands:

1. He is a growing Christian and leader in the home.
2. He has a sense of humor and is fun to be with.
3. He is a man of integrity and completely honest.
4. He is tender, gentle, and sensitive.
5. He prioritizes his family above his work or others.

All five of these are interesting. However, did you notice what was first on the list? "I want my husband to lead."

So you ask what women can do to help their husbands in being the leader God meant for them to be. Wives, allow me to share four suggestions with you:

First, **listen to your husband.** " . . . let every man be swift to hear . . ." (James 1:19). Many times women need to improve in this area of listening. One man said, "My wife speaks 140 words a minute with gusts up to 180." Another man said, "My wife and I had words last night; I just didn't get to use mine." The truth is most of us are not good listeners. Experts tell us 60 percent of the people cannot remember a single conversation they had yesterday. Larry King was correct when he said, "I have never learned anything while talking." When a wife listens to her husband, that sends the message that what he has to say is important.

Melissa Sounds headed up an organization called Mistresses Anonymous. It was a prostitution business. She made this statement to a local newspaper:

Ask any mistress; her man doesn't do anything but talk endlessly.
Mistresses are experts in the art of listening. People think a mistress has
a sex manual that keeps her man bewitched, but actually what she real-
ly has is the capacity to listen. Men have mistresses because they have
needs that they are unable to get met in their other lives. By needs, I
mean needs to communicate. They don't get these needs filled at home
because they see their wives when they are tired or worried about money
or early in the morning when they are both at their worst. They see
their wives at all the wrong times. Mistresses, however, see their men
when they are at the peak of their jobs, their day, and their energy and
motivation. A married woman takes time for her job, her kids, the
PTA, even her mother- in-law; but she does not make a special time to
listen to her husband. The mistress does.

When it comes to listening, I am saddened that the wrong group of women has learned it is important. I certainly am not advocating having an affair if your mate does not listen to you, but what I am imploring is for you to listen to your husband!

Below are two observations concerning listening to your husband:

A. When a man really needs to talk, he is not interested in your input. Women, when a man shares his problems, the last thing he wants is for you to rush right in and fix it for him. He knows what he needs to do to fix it. He does not need you for that! When you do that, it simply is saying to him, "I am smarter than you."

I remember one week I was struggling to find the right sermon—like I do many weeks. I was sharing my dilemma with my wife; and she said, "You are the greatest preacher in the world. I know you will get it." After that, I was ready to charge hell with a water pistol. Suppose she had said, "Baby, let me get a commentary and the *Strong's Concordance*; and we will put that sermon together." I would have felt like a failure.

B. Ladies, when your husband needs to share, he needs two things: one, appreciation for his struggle and two, affirmation that he can handle it.

Second, *do not shut down your husband's good ideas.* If every time your husband shares an idea, you are negative to it, guess what will begin to happen? He will not be sharing his ideas with you. Does your husband share ideas with you? Did he use to share ideas with you? How did you respond?

Jane Hill clearly understood this aspect of a wife's role. Over Jane's objections, her husband, the late E. V. Hill, once invested his family's scarce resources in the purchase of a service station. Jane opposed the decision because she knew her husband lacked the time and expertise to oversee the investment. She was right; the station went broke. When E. V. called to say he had lost the station, Jane could have said, "I told you so" and crushed his spirit. He could have been humiliated in that moment of vulnerability. Instead she said, "If you smoked and drank, you would have lost as much as you lost in the service station. So it's six in one hand and a half dozen in the other. Let's forget it."

A wife can make or break a man. If she believes in her husband and has confidence in his leadership, he typically gains the confidence he needs to take risks and use his assets wisely.

Third, *allow your husband to lead.* The Bible says, "And the LORD God took the man, and put him into the garden of Eden to dress it and to keep it" (Genesis 2:15). Even in the beginning of time, God placed a desire in man to work and lead. That is why God did not have to tell man to lead because it is natural for a man to lead.

Now let me show you what is not natural. The Bible says, "Unto the woman he said, I will greatly multiply thy sorrow and thy conception; in sorrow thou shalt bring forth children; and thy desire *shall* be to thy husband, and he shall rule over thee" (Genesis 3:16). Because of the fall of Adam and Eve in the Garden, God said there would be pain in childbirth and submission to her husband's leadership. By nature, Eve was independent; and this is why it is difficult for many women to allow their husbands to lead.

Women, you must provide a vacuum in order for your husband to lead. I am convinced there are women in America that neither Winston Churchill nor Norman Schwarzkopf could lead. These types will not allow their husbands to lead. This also explains why a man will go to work, church, or a civic club and be an exceptional leader. God placed a desire in man to lead. If he cannot do it at home, he will do it somewhere else.

If your husband is not the leader he should be, let me encourage you to not focus on his leadership but focus on your ability to be led. Again, you must provide the vacuum for him to lead.

Fourth, *admire your husband. Admire* means "to regard with wonder." The men reading this are saying, "Sounds great!" The women reading this are saying, "Get real!" Do you know the Bible says for wives to obey their husbands? *Obey* means "to pay close attention to." Every man needs admiration — especially from his wife.

Every Sunday morning, I stand in the foyer of our church and greet people as they exit. It is so encouraging to me when my parishioners share that the message was informative or inspirational. But all of those kind words pale in comparison to when my wife Barbara says, "Honey, you preached so well today." After that, I have the tartar sauce and I am ready to go hunt Moby Dick. Admiration is vital to every man. Even if your husband acts like he does not enjoy it, I assure you he does.

Let me give you six things to admire about your husband:

1. **Admire his appearance.** To everyone else, he may be a chunk; but let him be your hunk.

2. **Admire his mental capacity.** You may say, "My husband can't make good decisions." Well, he chose to marry you!

A husband asked his wife, "Why did you marry me? Was it my good looks, my muscular body, my wealth, my great personality?" "No," she said, "I married you for your brains." The husband began to smile and asked her to explain herself. The wife answered, "It is the small things that really count." **Admire his mental capacity!**

3. **Admire his competence on the job.** Learn about your husband's work and express interest in his work. Do not be like the lady who was asked by another lady what her husband did for a living. She stated, "He works with wires." I hope you know a little more about your husband's work than that he works with wires.

4. **Admire the manner in which he provides for his family.**

5. **Admire his physical strength.** No matter what the situation, you can find some way to compliment his physical strength. If nothing else, say, "Great, honey! You made it up the stairs!" I love it when my wife asks, "Will you open this jar of pickles?" I immediately think: *Just give them*

to Tarzan; and come hail or high water, I will open that jar of pickles.

6. **Admire his love for the Lord.** If he is not as far along in his relationship with Christ as you are, do not intimidate him! Many times a wife is deeper in her walk than her husband; and when she prays, she uses thirty-two verses of Scripture. Then she wonders why her husband will not pray with her. Can some of that knowledge, and encourage your husband to be the spiritual leader.

A man wrote a book and was very excited about getting it published. But as he started meeting with publishers, he became more and more discouraged because of the rejection that he encountered. After being turned down for the thirty-fifth time, he came home, threw his manuscript in the trash, and forbade his wife to get it out. His wife knew the material was quality, but she also knew she would be disobeying him by getting it out of the trash. How did she handle this dilemma? She simply took the trash can with the manuscript still in it to a publisher's office and said, "What is in here is gold, and I can't take it out; but you can." That is exactly what the publisher did and, in fact, published the book! The title was *The Power of Positive Thinking.* It has sold more than 30 million copies. I know Norman Vincent Peale was grateful that his wife Ruth believed in him as well as admired him. **Remember: listen to your husband, allow him to lead, and admire him – and he might just become the leader he needs to be.**

CHAPTER THREE

The Camels, the Couple, and the Commitment

Genesis 24:10-20

10. And the servant took ten camels of the camels of his master, and departed; for all the goods of his master were in his hand: and he arose, and went to Mesopotamia, unto the city of Nahor.

11. And he made his camels to kneel down without the city by a well of water at the time of the evening, even the time that women go out to draw water.

12. And he said, O LORD God of my master Abraham, I pray thee, send me good speed this day, and show kindness unto my master Abraham.

13. Behold, I stand here by the well of water; and the daughters of the men of the city come out to draw water:

14. And let it come to pass, that the damsel to whom I shall say, Let down thy pitcher, I pray thee, that I may drink; and she shall say, Drink, and I will give thy camels drink also: let the same

be she that thou hast appointed for thy servant Isaac; and thereby shall I know that thou hast shown kindness unto my master.

15.   And it came to pass, before he had done speaking, that, behold, Rebekah came out, who was born to Bethuel, son of Milcah, the wife of Nahor, Abraham's brother, with her pitcher upon her shoulder.

16.   And the damsel was very fair to look upon, a virgin, neither had any man known her: and she went down to the well, and filled her pitcher, and came up.

17.   And the servant ran to meet her, and said, Let me, I pray thee, drink a little water of thy pitcher.

18.   And she said, Drink, my lord: and she hasted, and let down her pitcher upon her hand, and gave him drink.

19.   And when she had done giving him drink, she said, I will draw water for thy camels also, until they have done drinking.

20.   And she hasted, and emptied her pitcher into the trough, and ran again unto the well to draw *water*, and drew for all his camels.

Everyone who knows me knows I am the biggest Tennessee Volunteer football fan. I believe God is a fan also; if not, why did He put that big orange ball up in the sky?

I am reminded of a young man who took a young lady on their first date to Neyland Stadium in Knoxville, Tennessee, to a football game. They were seated, watching the game when about half time a player ran out onto the field. The young man said to the young lady, "That will be our best man next year." She quickly responded, "That's a strange way to propose, but I accept!"

I was recently asked what Uncle Sam, a rooster, and an old maid have in common. I said I had no clue. The person asking said, "Uncle Sam says, 'Yankee Doodle do'; a rooster says, 'Cockle doodle do'; and an old maid says, 'Any old dud will do.' "

These are all humorous stories, but I am convinced God has a better plan for bringing the right person into our lives. Allow me to give you some background to the story that takes place in Genesis 24.

Abraham's wife, Sarah, had just died; and they had a son named Isaac. In the Old Testament, it was a father's responsibility to choose a wife for his son. (Yes, parents chose mates for their children. And as a parent of a growing-up-too-fast girl, I wish we would go back to Old Testament principles! Amen?) Abraham did not want his son to marry one of the pagan Canaanite girls where he lived. Therefore, he sent his eldest servant out with ten camels loaded with silver and gold to the land of Mesopotamia to find a godly bride for Isaac. Once the servant arrived near Mesopotamia, he stopped outside the city at a well to water his camels and there he prayed this prayer:

> *"Lord God, make me successful today. Here I am standing by the well and the girls of the city are coming out to draw water. I will ask a girl, 'May I please have a drink from your jar?' If she answers, 'Have a drink and I will also water your camels,' that will be the sign you have chosen her for Isaac's bride."*

Before he had completed his prayer, a beautiful girl named Rebekah came to draw water and offered him a drink as well as offered his camels water. God used camels to connect a couple. There are three important lessons we learn from this story:

First, **marry the right person.** Zig Ziglar was seated on an airplane and noticed the gentleman seated beside him had his wedding band on the wrong finger. Mr. Ziglar kindly mentioned to the gentleman that he noticed it. The man said, "I know it is. I married the wrong woman."

One of the saddest counseling sessions I have ever had in better than twenty years of ministry was with a lady who was planning to divorce her husband. With tears in her eyes, she said, "I have been miserable for twenty years of my marriage. A few days before my wedding day, God told me not to marry this man: but I brushed it off and went ahead with the plans. I have experienced a miserable marriage because of my decision."

Friend, it is better to be single and want to be married than to be married and want to be single. Allow me to give you five steps to marrying the right person:

1. **Pray.** Simply ask God to send you the person He has for you. The Bible says we have not because we ask not. A lady walked into a men's department store and said to the sales lady, "I am looking for something wild and sexy in a pair of men's slacks." The sales lady responded, "Aren't we all!" **Pray before you start looking!**

2. **Look for godly qualities.** Abraham did not want his son Isaac to marry one of the pagan-worshipping girls in Canaan. He wanted Isaac to be equally yoked with a godly girl. If you are single and a Christian, you should only date a Christian! The Bible teaches that a Christian is not to be unequally yoked. (2 Corinthians 6:14) Christians should only marry Christians and usually only marry people that they date first. I do not believe in missionary dating. There are a lot of reasons for a Christian not to marry a non-Christian – one of those being, if you are a Christian and marry a non-Christian, you immediately get the devil for your father-in-law. (John 8:44) Notice also that Rebekah was a virgin. (Genesis 24:16) **Look for good qualities!**

3. **Ladies, make sure he can bring home the bacon!** The Bible says, "But if any provide not for his own, and specially for those of his own house, he hath denied the faith, and is worse than an infidel" (1 Timothy 5:8). Abraham was a smart man. When he sent his servant to find a wife for

his son, he loaded him down with gifts of silver and gold. He knew ladies like jewelry. He even sent Isaac's future mother-in-law a gift. A stroke of brilliance! A young husband said to his young bride, "I wish you could make biscuits like Mama." She quickly replied, "I wish you could bring home the dough like Daddy." **Ladies, if he can work and won't work, you don't need him!**

4. **Men, make sure she is not afraid to water the camels.** Every day Rebekah went out and fetched the water her family needed. She was not just some flashy girl. She knew something about reality. Young couples, please realize the whole dating process is a forest. Yes, while dating, we are on our best behavior. The person we are dating is oftentimes not the same person we marry. That person is at home locked up in the cage! When you marry a girl and all she knows how to do is make reservations, in a short time you will be in trouble. A recently married young girl was crying to her mother that her new husband was just not the same since they got back from their honeymoon. "Mom, he is using terrible four-letter words!" The mother asked what they were. The new bride said, "They are wash, cook, dust, and iron!"

5. **Wait on God.** Rebekah was not even looking for a husband when the Lord arranged for her marriage to Isaac. She was not in a singles bar but was simply watering the camels. I am convinced when you meet the person God has for you it will be at a time and place when you are least expecting it. Always remember, it is better to be single and want to be married than to be married and want to be single! **Wait on God!**

Second, **manifest the right personality.** When Rebekah offered to water the camels, do you realize the task she was undertaking? A camel would drink between twenty to thirty gallons of water. For ten camels, she was going to have to draw around 300 gallons! This was a huge job to say the least! I am convinced Rebekah had "the other person" mindset. She focused on doing for others. She knew when you give flowers to others it always leaves a fragrance in your hand. The secret to success in marriage is just not finding the right person but more importantly *being* the right person.

I encourage you not to be like the man who went shopping with his wife. After trying on a new dress, the woman asked her husband, "Does this dress make me look fat?" "No," he said, "your hips make you look fat."

A man was on an airplane and noticed the woman seated next to him had a large diamond ring on her finger. He mentioned to her how beautiful the ring was, and she told him it was the famous White Diamond. She added that even though it is a beautiful ring a dreaded curse goes along with it. The man asked, "What is the curse?" She answered, "Mr. White."

I believe the secret to marital happiness is instead of putting people in their place, put yourself in their place. I have confidence there are five things that each and every individual wants to receive:

1. **Encouragement.** The Bible says, ". . . Man shall not live by bread alone . . ." (Matthew 4:4). Sometimes we need a little buttering!

2. **Appreciation.** A thank you goes a long way.

3. **To be listened to.** One man said to another man, "My wife talks to herself all the time." The other man responded, "My wife does too; she just thinks I'm listening."

4. **To be understood.** People don't care how much you know until they know how much you care.

5. **Forgiveness.** I love the little poem:
   If you want your marriage to sizzle
   With love in the loving cup,
   Whenever you are wrong, admit it;
   Whenever you are right, shut up.

Think about yourself a minute. Do you want encouragement, appreciation, and forgiveness? Sure you do! Friend, the only way to receive these attributes is to give them. Begin manifesting the right personality today.

Third, **master the right priorities.** Once Rebekah decided that God wanted her to be the wife of Isaac, she began making plans to travel from Mesopotamia to Canaan. Her mother and brother said to her that she could not leave yet and asked her to stay at least ten more days. Her response to them was: "I will go." She realized the closest earthly relationship is the husband-and-wife relationship. She had the right priorities.

If you are married, your top priority is not your mother, father, children, or brothers and sisters. Your top priority is your mate! The Bible says, "Therefore shall a man leave his father and his mother, and shall cleave unto his wife: and they shall be one flesh" (Genesis 2:24).

I recently read Todd Duncan's book *The Power to Be Your Best.* In it, he shared five keys to a successful marriage:

1. **Honor your mate.** Brag on your mate in public.

2. **Be a meaningful communicator.** One lady said to me, "Pastor, I thought I married a communicating partner; but I married a couch that burps!"

3. **Appreciate each other's strengths and weaknesses.** In a survey of couples who had been married twenty-five years or more and who would marry the same person again, it was discovered that an overwhelming majority (84 percent) of them took their mates not only for better or worse but as they are! After all their years together, they claimed to strive to accept their mates just the way they are right now.

4. **Touch each other often.** Research by a West German insurance company reveals that a man who kisses his wife goodbye (and I mean really

kisses her goodbye) will live an average of five and a half years longer than those men who forgo this pleasant little way of departing. Fellows, your life is at stake here! Not only that, but the men who do this earn an average of 20 to 30 percent more money than those who have to leave home under their own power. So, yes, there are lots of benefits to this way of departing!

5. **Bond together by being together.** My wife and I recently had an experience we will cherish forever. We traveled to Colorado Springs, Colorado, and met with Dr. James Dobson of Focus on the Family. I had a list of questions I wanted to ask the man I believe has done more for the spiritual health and moral well-being of the family than any other individual in America. The first question I asked was: "What do you perceive to be the greatest threat to families today?" I will never forget his answer. He said, "I could talk about alcoholism, drug abuse, infidelity, and the other common causes of divorce; but there is another curse that accounts for more breakups than the others combined. It is the simple matter of overcommitment and the tyranny of the urgent."

Husbands and wives who fill their lives with never-ending volumes of work are too exhausted to take walks together, to share their deeper feelings, to understand and meet each other's needs. They are even too worn out to have a meaningful sexual relationship because fatigue is a destroyer of desire.

I am convinced it is one thing to keep a marriage going but another thing to keep it flowing. Is yours just going, or is it flowing? I have had the privilege of traveling this world over through my pulpit ministry. I have been in a diversity of homes, different races, different ages, different backgrounds, and different economic standards. I have been in homes where you could see the ground below, and I have been in homes where you could see the stars and the moon through the ceiling. But I have never met a truly fulfilled and contented person who was not fully committed to only one person – no matter what the status of their life was. Many men reach forty and think they need two twenty year olds. But men, **you do not!** God did not wire you for two twenties.

The story of David Ireland really sums up what I am trying to say. He wrote *Letters to an Unborn Child* to his child still in the womb of his wife because he was dying from a crippling neurological disease. He knew he might never get the opportunity to see, hold, rock, or kiss his child or take his child to a ball game or a movie. A child he might never shoot baskets with, take to the circus, or comfort after a bad dream. He desperately wanted his child to know that, whether dead or alive, Daddy loves his son or daughter. And with that in mind, David wrote the following:

Your mother is very special. Few men know what it is like to receive appreciation for taking their wives out to dinner when it entails what it does for us. It means that she has to dress me, shave me, brush my teeth, comb my hair, wheel me out of the house and down the steps, open the garage, open the car door, take the pedals off my wheelchair, stand me up, sit me on the seat of the car, turn my legs around so that I am comfortable, fold the wheelchair, put it into the car, go around to the driver's side, start it, back up, get out, close the garage, get back in the car, and then drive to the restaurant. Then it starts all over again. She gets out of the car, takes out the wheelchair, unfolds it, opens my door, spins me around, stands me up, sits me in the wheelchair, puts the legs back on the wheelchair, pushes the pedals down, closes and locks the car, wheels me into the restaurant, finds a table, takes the pedals back off, so I will be more comfortable; and she then feeds me through the entire meal. When it is over, she pays the bill, pushes the wheelchair out to the car again, and begins the same routine.

When it is all over – finished – with great warmth, she'll say, "Honey, thank you for taking me out to dinner." I never quite know how to answer.

CHAPTER FOUR

Genesis 2:19-25

19. And out of the ground the LORD God formed every beast of the field, and every fowl of the air; and brought them unto Adam to see what he would call them: and whatsoever Adam called every living creature, that was the name thereof.

20. And Adam gave names to all cattle, and to the fowl of the air, and to every beast of the field; but for Adam there was not found an help meet for him.

21. And the LORD God caused a deep sleep to fall upon Adam, and he slept: and he took one of his ribs, and closed up the flesh instead thereof;

22. And the rib, which the LORD God had taken from man, made he a woman, and brought her unto the man.

23. And Adam said, This is now bone of my bones, and flesh of my flesh: she shall be called Woman, because she was taken out of Man.

24. Therefore shall a man leave his father and his mother, and shall cleave unto his wife: and they shall be one flesh.

25. And they were both naked, the man and his wife, and were not ashamed.

A fictitious story read, "One day an angel came to Adam and said, 'I have a proposition for you.'" Adam said, "Let's hear it." The angel said, "I want to give you a woman." Adam asked, "What is that, and what will she do?" The angel answered, "Well, when you come in from the garden, she will meet you at the door dressed beautifully. She will then serve you a delicious hot meal. She will massage your body after a hard day's work. She will then prepare your water to bathe in and be at your beck and call to meet every request." After hearing all of this, Adam asked, "What is all this going to cost me?" The angel said, "Your right arm and a leg." Adam asked, "What can I get for just a rib?" With that, he got a woman!

Who is better: a man or a woman? The answer is: "Yes." A man is better at being a man, and a woman is better at being a woman. The Bible says, "There is neither Jew nor Greek, there is neither bond nor free, there is neither male nor female: for ye are all one in Christ Jesus" (Galatians 3:28).

Adam had just named all the animals (no doubt he had the company of thousands of animals), but his life was still not complete. We must understand that God did not give man a woman to compete with him but to complete him. Notice that Adam said, "I finally have someone like me." (Genesis 2:23) He liked the fact that they were alike but also liked the fact that they were different. (Genesis 2:25)

It is very important for us to realize that God made man and woman different. I would like to use generalities and compare how men and women are different. Notice I said generalities. There will be some exceptions; but for the most part, these comparisons will define how the sexes are different.

First, **the Beauty and the Beast:**

God made men stronger than women (1 Peter 3:7), and He had a reason for that. God placed man in the garden "to dress it and to keep it" (Genesis 2:15). God's plan was for man to be the protector and provider for the home. Scores of men need to get off their seat, on their feet, out in the street, and bring in the meat.

Now Eve was the life giver. She was not meant to till the ground. Men are not meant to bare children, and women are not meant to fight wars. Did you know that 40 percent of man's body is muscle compared to 25 percent in a woman's body? The other 15 percent are a thin layer of cellulite, and that is why it is easier for a woman to gain weight than a man. Therefore, it is harder for her to lose it than for him.

Man has $1^1/_2$ gallons of blood in his body, but a woman has only 4/5 of a gallon. Man has nearly 50 percent more blood. This explains why a woman has cold feet. This also explains when the temperature at church is just right for men, but the women are freezing.

Allow me to share a few more differences. Men have a larger lung capacity, but women have a stronger immune system. Yes, men, women will outlive us.

One other difference that women already know is that men have thicker skulls than women. All the women said, "Amen!"

Second, **the Romantic and the Mechanic:**

Men are work oriented. Remember that God put man in the garden to keep it; and it was the woman who had the babies. Women are relationship oriented. If you don't believe this, notice the difference in what men and women read. Women read *How to Develop Intimacy in Your Marriage: Five Keys to a Deeper Romance.* What do men read? *Getting Better Gas Mileage* or *Remodeling the Garage.*

Have you ever noticed how high school boys and girls carry their books differently? The girls hold their books up very close to their chests. The boys hold theirs nonchalantly on the side – if they carry them at all.

Another difference between men and women I have noticed is that when a woman goes to the restroom she rarely goes alone. When my wife and I have been with other couples for dinner, one lady would ask the other: "Would you like to go to the restroom?" Now, men, I don't know about you; but after many years of socializing and fellowshipping with men, a man has never asked me if I would like to go to the restroom! Thank you, Lord! The woman is the romantic by nature, and the man is the mechanic.

The Song of Solomon is a great book on how men and women are different. It is the account of Solomon's relationship with his Shulamite bride. Notice how they were different. First, the bride was motivated by romance. She said, "He brought me to the banqueting house, and his banner over me was love. Sustain me with cakes of raisins, refresh me with apples, for I am lovesick. His left hand is under my head, and his right hand embraces me" (Song of Solomon 2:4-6, New King James).

Now notice what motivated Solomon. He said, "Your lips are like a strand of scarlet, and your mouth is lovely. Your temples behind your veil are like a piece of pomegranate. Your neck is like the tower of David, built for an armory, on which hang a thousand bucklers, all shields of mighty men, Your two breasts are like two fawns, twins of a gazelle, which feed among the lilies" (Song of Solomon 4:3-5, New King James). He was not motivated by romance but by sight. What he saw turned him on!

The bottom line is that men need to work on being romantic. Men, allow me to give you ten romantic ideas:

1. Buy a bouquet of flowers or even a single rose – for no special occasion.

2. Get your loved one a card, or make one yourself.

3. Post a love note on a cereal box or the fridge. (I put a note to Barbara in the refrigerator once that read: "It may be cold in here, but my heart burns for you. Love, Benny")

4. Designate one night a week as "date night."

5. Spend twenty minutes together in bed before falling asleep to talk and cuddle.

6. Call just to say hello.

7. Say "I love you" often.

8. Bring home a favorite treat.

9. Communicate to your loved one what you find romantic.

10. Just hold hands.

Women, you need to try to keep yourself looking as good as possible. When he married you, you looked like Wonder Woman. Now when he comes home from work, he wonders if you are a woman! I have often been asked, "Is it a sin for a woman to wear makeup?" My response is usually: "It ought to be a sin for some women not to!" In other words, ladies, if you are not employed outside the home, stop a few minutes before he is scheduled to be home and freshen up a little. Comb your hair; put on clean clothes; a little perfume would help; and brush your teeth! Take a few minutes to catch your breath, and be ready for his arrival. By the way, it is biblical for a woman to take pride in her appearance. "Do not let your adornment be merely outward—arranging the hair, wearing gold, or putting on fine apparel—rather let it be the hidden person of the heart, with the incorruptible beauty of a gentle and quiet spirit, which is very precious in the sight of God" (1 Peter 3:3-4, NKJV).

Women, notice God spoke of the importance of inward and outward adorning. Keep yourself looking as good as possible for your mechanic, and he might become a romantic.

Third, **the Code Speaker and the Reporter:**

Men report the facts. A man comes home from work; and his wife says, "How was your day?" He answers, "Fine." Men, she wants more than fine! She wants details! The problem is that the average man speaks 12,500 words a day and the average woman speaks 25,000 words a day. When the man comes home from work, he has used up all of his words!

Many times my wife will ask: "How did your lunch go today?" I know exactly what she is asking: "Where did you go? Who did you go with? Who did you see? What did you eat?" She wants details! Many men need to learn to communicate with their wives and not just report the facts. The following story is a great example.

> *Wife:* Dear, the plumber didn't come to fix the leak behind the water heater today.
>
> *Husband:* Uh-huh.
>
> *Wife:* The pipe burst today and flooded the basement.
>
> *Husband:* Quiet. It's third down and goal to go.
>
> *Wife:* Some of the wiring got wet and almost electrocuted Fluffy.
>
> *Husband:* Darn it! Touchdown.
>
> *Wife:* The vet says he'll be better in a week.
>
> *Husband:* Can you get me a Coke?
>
> *Wife:* The plumber told me that he was happy that our pipe broke because now he can afford to go on vacation.
>
> *Husband:* Aren't you listening? I said I could use a Coke!
>
> *Wife:* And Stanley, I'm leaving you. The plumber and I are flying to Acapulco in the morning.

Husband: Can't you please stop all that yakking and get me a Coke? The trouble around here is that nobody ever listens to me.

Now women are code speakers. I have learned not to listen to what they say but what they mean. Let me give you some examples.

A man asks his wife, "What's wrong?" She says, "Nothing." That probably means everything is wrong. Women speak in codes.

A woman dresses up and asks her husband, "Do I look nice?" "Yes" is not the answer she wants; the answer is: "You look absolutely beautiful!"

A woman says to her husband, "I don't have anything to cook for dinner tonight." The husband replies, "Well, go to the grocery store and get something." I can assure you that was not the answer she was looking for. She more than likely wanted him to say, "Why don't we go out for supper?" Yes, women speak in codes!

A synopsis of all of this is that men need to learn to communicate and women need to say what they really mean.

Fourth, **the Cry Baby and the Snowman:**

In 1981, Roger Sperry won the Nobel Peace Prize in science and medicine for the following discovery. He discovered that during the sixteenth and twenty-sixth weeks of a woman's pregnancy, if she were carrying a boy, there will be a chemical reaction that slows down the development of the right side of the brain. He confirmed what we already know: men are brain damaged. This does not happen in pregnancies with a girl in the womb. What is interesting is the right side of our brain produces emotion and the left side produces logic. This explains why women tend to be more emotional than men and why men seem to be more stern.

This also explains why women cry more than men. After almost twenty years of marriage, I have learned that when I come home and my wife is crying not to ask, "Why are you crying?" Nor do I say, "You shouldn't be crying" or "Quit crying." But rather I put my arm around her and cry with her. Then after about ten minutes, I ask, "By the way, what are we crying about?" Women are right-brain emotion, and we can't change it!

Years ago a couple in my church found out that she was pregnant with the son they had wanted so badly. They were ecstatic! Soon they were told that the child she was carrying was going to die because of congenital abnormalities. They were devastated, and she cried at any given moment. Not only are the hormones in over-drive during this time, but hearing this news was extremely emotional in itself. She and her husband were going to town one day, and she began to cry. He looked at her and said words that she will never forget. He said, "Just quit crying about it." Notice the left-brain logic. Later the wife shared with me that it was not until he cried with her that the two of them could deal with God's plan together.

Katie was just seven years old when she taught her dad a lesson. One afternoon Katie asked if she could play with her friend next door. Dad told her it would be fine as long as she was home by six o'clock. Unfortunately, Katie was not home by six. Dad grew a little upset when he had to call and ask for Katie to be sent home. When she got home a half-hour late, her dad asked, "Didn't you hear me tell you to be home by six o'clock?" She answered, "Yes, but my friend's doll broke." Her dad mellowed a bit and said, "Oh, I see. So you stayed to help her fix it." "No," Katie said, "I stayed to help her cry."

I am convinced that many men are trying to fix everything when many times women do not want a Mr. Fix-it. They simply want compassion for their hurts and struggles.

I also encourage wives to try to understand that men have left-brain logic. Yes, they can be snowmen; but God made them this way. Let me give a great example.

On November 22, 1963, when President John F. Kennedy was assassinated, what was the response of women in America? "Poor Jackie. Little John John and Caroline will never know their dad." Right-brain emotion. What were the men in America thinking? "Who will run this country?" Left-brain logic.

Is either side right or wrong? No. They are just different, and husbands and wives must understand the difference.

Fifth, **Danielle Steele and Alexander the Great:**

Men are goal oriented, and they want to conquer. I realized this when I was only ten years of age. I was playing a game of checkers and was obviously going to lose; so I pushed the board over, spilling all of the checkers onto the floor. I then began hitting the person I was playing with. It was then when my stepfather grabbed me and said, "If you ever do that again to your grandmother, I will take you to the woodshed and there will be bloodshed." Men want to conquer because they want admiration.

Our church began a men's basketball team. We finished the season with a perfect record. We were 0-11, and we were not as good as our record. Rarely, and I do mean rarely, did I score. But even a clock is right twice a day, and occasionally I would score a basket. Guess who was the first person I looked for in the crowd after scoring? You guessed it. My wife! All men want and need admiration. This explains why men want to conquer.

Women want affection. They want holding hands, kissing, and embracing in public and in private.

A freelance reporter from *The New York Times* was interviewing Marilyn Monroe. She was aware of Marilyn's past and the fact that during her early years Marilyn had been shuffled from one foster home to another. The reporter asked Marilyn, "Did you ever feel loved by any of the foster families with whom you lived?"

"Once," Marilyn replied, "when I was about seven or eight. The woman I was living with was putting on makeup, and I was watching her. She was in a happy mood, so she reached over and patted my cheeks with her rouge puff. For that moment, I felt loved by her."

Marilyn Monroe had tears in her eyes when she remembered this event. Why? The touch lasted only a few seconds, and it happened years before. It was even done in a casual, playful way – not in an attempt to communicate great warmth or meaning. But as small an act as it was, it was like pouring buckets of love and security on the parched life of a little girl starved for affection.

Many wives in America are also starving for affection because many husbands have never realized their need for affection. The bottom line is that men love conquering and women love connecting.

In 1995, Christopher Reeve had it all. He was married to his best friend Dana. He had three wonderful children. He and his family enjoyed their estate in beautiful Westchester County, New York.

It seemed that he could do anything he put his mind to. He was an accomplished pianist who composed classical music. He was an avid outdoorsman and a superb athlete. Of course most know him as an actor—particularly as "Superman." He was also an expert sailor, a licensed pilot, an excellent skier, a scuba diver, and a horseman.

But on May 27, 1995 during the cross-country portion of a riding competition, Christopher Reeve was thrown from his horse Buck. He crashed head first into a fence that his horse refused to jump over and then fell to the ground. He sustained an injury to his spine at the first and second vertebrae. His breathing stopped. He was paralyzed from the neck down. If the paramedics had not arrived within minutes, he would not have survived.

Reeve has no memory of the fall. He remembers the time he spent in the stables a few minutes before his ride. The next thing he remembers is waking a few days later in the intensive care unit in the University of Virginia Hospital.

During those few intense days, he was kept alive by being on a respirator. The doctors literally, surgically reattached his head to his spine. The damage Reeve sustained is sometimes called "hangman's injury." Reeve later said, "It was as if I'd been hanged, cut down, and sent to rehab." He was given a 50 percent chance of surviving.

After the ordeal, Reeve shared, "When I first awoke and they shared with me what my condition was, I felt I was no longer a human being. Then my wife, Dana, came into my room and knelt down to the level of my bed. We made eye contact. I said, 'Maybe this isn't worth it. Maybe I should just check out.' While she was crying, she said, 'But you are still you and I love you.' *That saved my life!*'

Truly, men are Alexander the Greats and women are Danielle Steeles.

CHAPTER FIVE

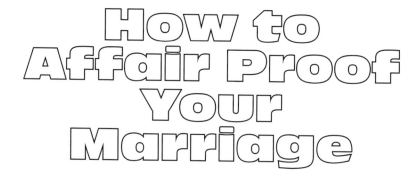

1 Corinthians 7:1-5

1. Now concerning the things whereof ye wrote unto me: *It is good* for a man not to touch a woman.

2. Nevertheless, *to avoid* fornication, let every man have his own wife, and let every woman have her own husband.

3. Let the husband render unto the wife due benevolence: and likewise also the wife unto the husband.

4. The wife hath not power of her own body, but the husband: and likewise also the husband hath not power of his own body, but the wife.

5. Defraud ye not one the other, except *it be* with consent for a time, that ye may give yourselves to fasting and prayer; and come together again, that Satan tempt you not for your incontinency.

In order to understand these Scriptures, we must understand the historical background of Corinth. In Corinth was the Temple of Aphrodite (Greek goddess of love and beauty). It towered over the city like a dark cloud. This temple was like most heathen temples. Sex was a religion. There were 1,000 so-called vestal virgins in the temple. You could get food, drink, and sex. Those women were no more than prostitutes. Sex was carried on in the name of religion. Fornication and adultery were rampant. In order to address the problem, Paul penned the Scriptures we just read.

Two thousand years have passed, but I assure you that immorality is still a severe issue destroying thousands of homes annually. I am convinced our churches have been silent too long! It is time for the churches of America to address this epidemic! Allow me to give you five reasons we should discuss the sexual relationship in church:

1. Only 30 percent of the men in America claim to be sexually faithful.

2. By age forty, 55 percent of all women in America will have had an affair.

3. God's very first command to humankind was in regard to sex. (Genesis 1:28)

4. People must be taught in this area. (Hosea 4:6) A father said to his fourth grader, "Son, I would like to talk to you about sex." The young boy responded, "Sure, Dad. What do you need to know?" People are going to learn about sex somewhere. Wouldn't it be better to come from the Bible and the Church than from the restroom walls?

5. We should not be ashamed to discuss what God was not ashamed to create. Yes, sex was God's idea. It is wonderful, and most of us are here because of it!

Marriage is God's provision for a sexual relationship. The sexual relationship is very sacred and very special and is meant to be between a husband and his wife. If you are not married, God is not keeping you from sex, but He is keeping sex for you. It is a spiritual union in which two people become one flesh. How do we keep our marriages affair proof? Let us look at three steps:

1. A Reading That Is Regular

The material that we take into our hearts and minds is vitally important. One national magazine recently reported that in one month one pornographic site received more than 6 million hits. Did you know that six out of ten men admit they have a sizeable problem with sexual immorality? If you are a man, you may be thinking: *Well, I don't.* If so, good for you. I would love to meet you because you are stronger than Samson, godlier than David, and wiser than Solomon. Sexual temptation is an issue many men struggle with. I recently learned that men prefer to have sexual relations on days that begin with T: Tuesday, Thursday, Today, Tomorrow, Taturday, and Tunday. (Just kidding!) The truth is that God has given men a God-given impulse that must be God-guided. The Scripture tells us: "For the commandment is a lamp; and the law is light; and reproofs of instruction are the way of life: To keep thee from the evil woman, from the flattery of the tongue of a strange woman" (Proverbs 6:23-24). The Word will keep you from sin, and sin will keep you from the Word. Remember, the Bible says, "Thy word have I hid in mine heart, that I might not sin against thee" (Psalm 119:11.)

Dr. Howard Hendricks interviewed 600 religious leaders who fell because of sexual immorality; they all had three things in common. First, they did not have private devotions. Second, they were not accountable. Third, they never thought it would happen to them.

I want to encourage you to have a reading that is regular. We all need a daily devotion time in which we read and study the Word of God. One of the things I have done that has helped me in my devotion time is to read a Proverb that correlates with the day of the month. There are thirty-one chapters. (Of course, you will need to read an extra chapter on the shorter months.) Great nuggets for living are found in these! To keep your marriage affair proof, you need a reading that is regular.

2. A Removing That Is Right

Did you know the Bible says, "Flee fornication . . ." (1 Corinthians 6:18) and "Flee also youthful lusts . . ." (2 Timothy 2:22)? Do you remember what Joseph did when his boss's wife made advances to him? He ran! Yes, he lost his coat; but he kept his character. Why did he not simply pray? I know why. The spirit is willing, but the flesh is weak. James Dobson said, "We must never underestimate the power of sexual chemistry existing between an attractive, needy, available woman and virtually any man on the face of the earth." We must realize that almost every affair begins as an innocent friendship. It is extremely important that we remove ourselves from places that would be tempting and questionable. I am convinced that when we speak of integrity and character Billy Graham personifies these qualities. He said, "Early in our marriage, Ruth and I decided I would never be alone with another woman in my office, our car, or out somewhere without a third party." Great advice!

Allow me to give you some warning signs that you may be heading toward an affair:

1. Do you look forward to an appointment with a certain person?
2. Had you rather see someone else more than your mate?
3. Do you find yourself making unnecessary phone calls?
4. Do you look for him or her in group settings?
5. Does he or she make you feel young and foolish?
6. Do you fantasize about someone other than your mate?

I think many times when we flee temptation we have a tendency to leave a forwarding address. I want to encourage you to realize God will not do for you that which you can do for yourself. Remember, He said, ". . . if thy right hand offend thee, cut it off . . ." (Matthew 5:30). Not that He would. I implore you to remove yourself from the place of temptation.

What is triggering your temptation? Is it a certain person? Stay away from him or her! Is it a movie? Turn it off! Do you know what a hypocrite is? A hypocrite is a person who complains about the sex, nudity, and violence on his VCR. Is it a certain type of music? Change the station! You will never change that which you are unwilling to confront. Leo Tolstoy was correct when he said, "Everyone thinks of changing the world, but no one thinks of changing himself." A great synopsis of what I am saying can be summed up in *An Autobiography in Five Short Paragraphs:*

1. I walk down the street. There is a deep hole in the sidewalk. I fall in. I am lost. I am helpless. It isn't my fault. It takes forever to find a way out.

2. I walk down the street. There is a deep hole in the sidewalk. I pretend I don't see it. I fall in. I can't believe I'm in the same place, but it isn't my fault. It still takes a long time to get out.

3. I walk down the street. There is a deep hole in the sidewalk. I see it is there. I still fall in. It's a habit. My eyes are open. I know where I am. It is my fault. I get out immediately.

4. I walk down the street. There is a deep hole in the sidewalk. I walk around it.

5. I walk down a different street.

3. A Relationship That Is Rich

The number one reason given for affairs in America is boredom in marriage. This tells me the best defense to an affair is a good offense. I love the story about the man who had been on a two-week trip and was picked up at the airport by his friend. His friend said to him, "What are your plans once you get home?" He answered, "Make love to my wife, and set my luggage down in that order." This is a humorous story, but marriage is God's provision for sexual fulfillment. We hear so much about "Safe Sex," but God never meant for it to be dangerous. I have the answer for sexually transmitted diseases: one man for one woman for one lifetime. The Bible tells us to avoid fornication (sex before marriage): "let every man have his own wife, and let every woman have her own husband" (1 Corinthians 7:2). The devil is lying to you when he tells you there is something better out there. The greatest sexual relationship takes place between a husband and a wife.

A new study commissioned by the Family Research Council of Washington, D.C., found that people most likely to report a high degree of satisfaction with their current sex life are married people who strongly believe that sex outside of marriage is wrong. The study found that 72 percent of these "married traditionalists" reported sexual satisfaction. This is 31 percent higher than unmarried nontraditionalists and 13 percent higher than married nontraditionalists. The study went on to show that sexually happy people also tend to go to church. Some two-thirds of the responders who attend church weekly are very satisfied with their sex lives – compared to barely half of those who never attend church.

The Bible also teaches we should not deprive our mate of sexual relations. "Let the husband render unto the wife due benevolence: and likewise also the wife unto the husband. The wife hath not power of her own body, but the husband: and likewise also the husband hath not power of his own body, but the wife" (1 Corinthians 7:3-4).

I love the story about the man who came to his wife's bed and had a glass of water and two Tylenols. She looked strangely at him and said, "I don't have a headache." Then he said, "Got ya!" The Bible says, "Drink waters out of thine own cistern, and running waters out of thine own well" (Proverbs 5:15). God wants husbands and wives to have a sexual relationship that is rich.

I travel and speak all over the country, and many times I am asked how I would like to be introduced. My answer is always the same. I ask them to tell the audience that I have been married to the same woman for almost twenty years. This is my greatest accomplishment; but I am keenly aware that the enemy would love to destroy my testimony, influence, and family.

Howard Hendricks said, "Satan will lie in the weeds for forty years to entrap one of God's servants." As a constant reminder of the importance of my faithfulness, I keep the following words taped in the leaf of my Bible:

- Your mate will experience the anguish of betrayal, shame, rejection, heartache, and loneliness. No amount of repentance will soften these blows.

- Your mate can never again say that you are a model of fidelity. Suspicion will rob her or him of trust.

- Your escapade(s) will introduce to your life and your mate's life the very real probability of a sexually transmitted disease.

- The total devastation your sinful actions will bring to your children is immeasurable. Their growth, innocence, trust, and healthy outlook on life will be severely and permanently damaged.

- The heartache you will cause your parents, your families, and your peers is indescribable.

- The embarrassment of facing other Christians who once appreciated you and trusted you will be overwhelming.

- If you were engaged in the Lord's work, you will suffer the immediate loss of your job and the support of those with whom you worked. The dark shadow will accompany you everywhere and forever. Forgiveness won't erase it.

- Your fall will give others license to do the same.

• The inner peace you enjoyed will be gone.

• You will never be able to erase the fall from your (or others') mind. This will remain indelibly etched on your life's record – regardless of your later return to your senses.

• The name of Jesus Christ, whom you once honored, will be tarnished, giving the enemies of faith further reason to sneer and jeer.

I remember a number of years ago watching Phyllis George interview Dallas Cowboy superstar Roger Staubach. It was a typical, dull sort of interview until Phyllis blindsided the quarterback with this question: "Roger, how do you feel when you compare yourself with Joe Namath who is so sexually active and has a different woman on his arm every time we see him?" How would *you* reply in front of several million people? We have all seen Staubach keep his cool in pressure game situations, and the tension in the air this time was just as great. But once again, Staubach kept his cool. "Phyllis," he said calmly, "I'm sure I'm as sexually active as Joe. The difference is that all of mine is with one woman."

On a regular basis, I remind my wife that I am faithful. Yes, to God, her, and our daughter. I am keenly aware that long before physical adultery takes place spiritual and emotional adultery have begun. I remember once telling my wife: "I had rather die than be unfaithful to you." Her response was: "Don't worry. If you are unfaithful, you will die!" Better low motivation than no motivation. Let's be faithful!

CHAPTER SIX

1 Corinthians 13:4-5

4. Charity suffereth long, *and* is kind; charity envieth not; charity vaunteth not itself, is not puffed up,

5. Doth not behave itself unseemly, seeketh not her own, is not easily provoked, thinketh no evil.

Oscar and Edith had just celebrated fifty years of marriage. They enjoyed a wonderful celebration with family and a host of friends, when Edith said to Oscar, "When you married me, you told me you loved me. But in all our years of marriage, you haven't said it again." Oscar replied, "Edith, I told you fifty years ago that I loved you; and if I ever change my mind, you will be the first to know."

In the day in which we live, so much is said on the subject of love. You hear remarks like: "We don't love each other anymore" or "We have fallen out of love." And this one: "I love her, but I am not in love with her."

What is love? Someone said love is a four-letter word composed of two consonants, L and V, and two fools, you and me. The world says love is something you feel. It is the "tingles." But I am convinced it is not something you feel but rather something you do. If it were something you feel, why would the Bible command husbands to love their wives (Ephesians 5:25) and for the older women to teach the younger women to love their husbands? (Titus 2:3-4) If it were a feeling, you would not have to be commanded to do it. You do not command someone to feel a certain way.

Love is an attitude (1 Corinthians 8:1); and love is an action. (1 Corinthians 13:3-4) Couples come to see me on a regular basis and say, "We don't love each other anymore." That is their way of saying: "We have no choice but divorce." They act as if the situation is beyond their control, and that might be true if love were a feeling. But love is an attitude and an action.

Couples can fall in love again. Yes, they just need to get back to the attitudes and actions that caused them to fall in love in the first place.

How can couples get back to that attitude and action? I am convinced that through words and behavior this can be achieved. Words are extremely powerful. They can build people up or pull them down. "Death and life are in the power of the tongue . . ." (Proverbs 18:21).

A man was looking under his bed for his shoe-shining kit when he noticed an unfamiliar box. When he opened it, he saw six golf balls and $2600 in cash. He immediately went to his wife and asked her if she knew anything about the box. She hesitated at first and then said, "Yes, as a Christian, I must be honest. It is mine." He looked puzzled and asked what was up with all this money and why the golf balls. She explained, "Honey, I don't want to hurt your feelings; but every time you were a lousy lover, I put a golf ball in the box." He thought a moment and asked, "Well, I'm not too disappointed after twenty years; but what is all the money about? When I was great, did you put a dollar in the box?" "Oh no," she said. "When I got a dozen golf balls, I sold them." Words can pick us up or pull us down! Allow me to give you some words we need to say to our mates:

1. Compliments

The Bible says, "Let no corrupt communication proceed out of your mouth, but that which is good to the use of edifying, that it may minister grace unto the hearers" (Ephesians 4:29).

A man had his head lying on his wife's lap when she removed his glasses and said, "With your glasses off, you look just like you did when we married." He said, "With my glasses off, you do too." She knew how to give compliments; he did not.

I recently expressed to my wife that I wished I were younger and asked her if she knew why. She said she did not. I said, "So I could be married to you longer."

Mark Twain said he could survive two months on one single compliment. **Learn to be complimentary!**

2. Kindness

The Bible says, ". . . be ye kind one to another . . ." (Ephesians 4:32). I am convinced kindness is always important – especially if you have been hurt. The Bible says, "A soft answer turneth away wrath . . ." (Proverbs 15:1). I learned a long time ago that cold hearts and hot heads do not solve anything. When volume goes up, communication goes down. Whoever said, "It is nice to be important, but it is more important to be nice" was correct. **Be kind!**

3. Requests rather than demands

The Bible teaches that love does not demand its own way. (1 Corinthians 13:5) In a successful marriage, you hear questions like: "Could we do this? Is this possible? What do you think? Do you mind?" I am talking about requests rather demands.

A man went to a seminar on male superiority. He was extremely excited about the information he had learned and attempted to bring the information home to his wife. He demanded she sit down while he explained to her the things that were soon going to be different around their house. He started with: "Tonight you will serve me dinner in the living room; you will remove my boots; and then you will run my bath water. Do you know who will then dress me?" "Yes," she said, "the undertaker!" Remember, the secret is requests rather than demands.

I love ball games. I especially like college football games. I especially like attending them. But in almost twenty years of marriage, I have never told my wife I was going to a game. I always asked her if she would mind if I were to go. Yes, I am the leader of my home, but I realize I will not enjoy the game without her blessing. And by the way; she has never opposed my going to a game but rather encouraged me to go. I may be "some dumb" but not "plumb dumb." Remember, *Happy Wife, Happy Life!* Requests are better than demands.

4. Words of acceptance

Suppose a man comes home after a hard day at work (I assure you there will be days like that) and wants to share his struggles with his wife. She is constantly interrupting and giving advice during his talking. He finally just gives up and quits speaking. Wives, I assure you if he shares his struggles with you he is not wanting you to fix the problem. He is wanting acceptance. He is wanting you to simply listen, understand his situation, and assure him he will overcome it.

The same is true with a wife when she says, "I don't feel loved." What do we do? We immediately respond, "What about the dress I bought you two years ago? What about the nice dinner I took you out for last summer?" We are condemning her feelings. It would be much better if we would ask, "Why do you feel that way?" That shows we are accepting the way she feels. Words of acceptance are vital to every relationship.

5. Present-tense words

With this I am talking about keeping no record when we have been wronged. One man said to another, "When my wife becomes upset, she becomes so historical." The other man said, "You mean she becomes so hysterical?" "No," he said, "I mean historical. She keeps bringing up the past."

I learned a long time ago you can not saw sawdust. Paul said, "Brethren, I count not myself to have apprehended: but this one thing I do, forgetting those things which are behind, and reaching forth unto those things which are before" (Philippians 3:13).

We have a choice. We can reflect on the scars or reach for the stars. Lines from one of my favorite poems says,

> *Though we cannot go back and make a brand new start,*
> *We can begin now and make a brand new end.*

Not only can we fall in love again through words but also through our behavior and actions. Yes, our actions are even louder than our words.

> *A bell is not a bell until you ring it.*
> *A song is not a song until you sing it.*
> *Love is not put in your heart to stay,*
> *It is not love until you give it away.*

The Bible says, "My little children, let us not love in word, neither in tongue; but in deed and in truth" (1 John 3:18). The type of behavior we should exemplify is found in 1 Corinthians 13:4-5:

1. Patient behavior

Anyone who knows me knows this is not one of my virtues, but I assure you I am working on it. I am the guy that paces the floor while my wife is getting ready. I heard about one man who each Sunday would get ready for church and then go out into the car and honk the horn. He always complained that his wife took too long to get ready. Finally, one Sunday he went out and began honking the horn. His wife came out and got into the car. There was only one problem. She was completely naked! Needless to say, he doesn't honk the horn anymore.

I also know many wives who complain that their husbands won't finish projects at their homes. Allow me to make two observations.

First, a nagging woman is like a continuous raindrop. (Proverbs 27:15)

Second, if you are patient and try to compliment him on the projects he has completed, I assure you he will get more accomplished.

Patient behavior is the key.

2. Kind behavior

I am convinced that many times we are kinder to the waitress, the convenience store worker, and our co-workers than we are to our mate. One Sunday I spoke about being kind to your mate and a man who has a history of being very unkind was challenged by the message. The following Monday he left work early, purchased flowers and candy for his wife, and showed up with them at their home. When she came to the door and saw him there smiling, she began to cry and said, "Everything has gone wrong today. The baby has cried all day; the dishwasher won't work; the commode won't flush; and you come home drunk!" You may want to begin your kindness in small steps if you haven't had a history of kind behavior.

Husbands, I encourage you to do acts of kindness. Call your wife in the middle of the day – just to tell her you are thinking of her and that you love her. Send her love notes. Many times when I am away, I send Barbara a note, telling her of a special gift I hid in the house for her. Yes, it takes some time and thought; but I assure you it is well worth the effort.

Wives, I encourage you to do acts of kindness for your husband. Be excited to see him when he gets home from work. Encourage him in his recreation. Drop him a note, and thank him for being a good provider. Many times when I am away from home speaking, I find cards in my luggage and in my suit pockets from Barbara. Little acts of kindness go a long way.

3. Humble behavior

The text tells us that love vaulteth not itself. This teaches us that humble behavior is important to any relationship. If we carry ourselves in a humble fashion, we will have no problem saying, "I'm sorry." If you have a successful marriage, you will have to learn to say these two words on a regular basis.

I also learned that a more mature person in any relationship will always be the first to say, "I'm sorry." That person has realized the issue is not *who* is right but rather *what* is right.

The Bible also says in our text that love is not easily provoked. If you are constantly being offended, the problem could lie with the pride you have built up in your heart and not with the other person. Humble behavior is vital to any relationship.

4. Unselfish behavior

The text says love seeketh not her own. Many couples share with me that they have separate bank accounts. I personally do not recommend this because it can breed selfish behavior. My philosophy is: what is mine is ours, and what is yours is ours. It is very interesting to me that we want to be one flesh with two bank accounts.

There is a story about a man and a wife who were celebrating their golden wedding anniversary – fifty years of married life. Having spent most of the day with relatives and friends at a big party given in their honor, they were back home again. They decided before retiring to have a little snack of tea with bread and butter. They went into the kitchen where the husband opened up a new loaf of bread and handed the end piece (the heel) to his wife whereupon she exploded! She said, "For fifty years, you have been dumping the heel of bread on me. I will not take it anymore; this is a lack of concern for me and what I like." On and on she went in the bitterest of terms for his offering her the heel of the bread. The husband was absolutely astonished at her tirade. When she had finished, he said to her quietly, "But it's my favorite piece."

Unselfish behavior is important! You may be thinking all this sounds great, but what if you have loved in attitude and actions and it is not reciprocated. What would you do? You are correct in part of your observation. The Bible says, "Husbands, love your wives, even as Christ also loved the church, and gave himself for it" (Ephesians 5:25). Christ exemplified the ultimate act of love when He died for His wife on Calvary's cross. Still we neglect and reject His love. One can love in words and deeds, yet people still have a choice because of their free will. But I assure you that you will have a better chance of a positive response if you exemplify love in your words and actions.

A man went to a realtor and said, "I want to get rid of my dilapidated, run-down house." The realtor asked the man to describe it to him, so he could write it up in the ad. The man told him about his house, and the realtor read back what the man had described: "For Sale: Beautiful 3-bedroom, 2-bath brick home, great lawn, fruit trees, new roof, central heating and air." The man yelled out, "Stop! All my life I've been looking for a house like that!" He didn't realize what he had.

I am convinced this is also true with numerous couples. If you will try the right words and the right actions, you might realize what you want is just what you already have!

CHAPTER SEVEN

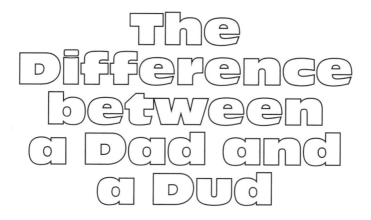

Psalm 128:1-6

1. Blessed is every one that feareth the LORD; that walketh in his ways.

2. For thou shalt eat the labour of thine hands: happy shalt thou be, and it shall be well with thee.

3. Thy wife shall be as a fruitful vine by the sides of thine house: thy children like olive plants round about thy table.

4. Behold, that thus shall the man be blessed that feareth the LORD.

5. The LORD shall bless thee out of Zion: and thou shalt see the good of Jerusalem all the days of thy life.

6. Yea, thou shalt see thy children's children, and peace upon Israel.

Four-year-old Tommy got a puppy on his birthday. He named it Laddie. He and the pup became friends immediately. Unfortunately, the pup proved to be unmanageable. He refused to be house broken; disobeyed every order; and seemed to enjoy destroying socks, slippers, carpets, and furniture. The mother finally ran out of patience and took the dog to relatives far out in the country. She was a bit leery about breaking the news to young Tommy. She decided to wait until breakfast. Speaking softly, she said, "I sent Laddie away, so you won't ever see him again." To her surprise, Tommy said, "No big deal, Mom. Don't worry about it!" With that being said, he went out to play.

A few minutes later, Tommy ran back in the house, sobbing uncontrollably. Hysterically, he said, "Laddie's gone! Where's my dog? I want my dog!" "Son," his mom said, "I told you at breakfast that Laddie was gone, and you seemed just fine. What's the problem?" "Laddie?!" the boy answered. "I thought you said Daddy."

This is a humorous story, but the truth of the matter is there is a great difference in fathering a child and in being a father to a child. Psalm 128 shows us five differences between a dad and a dud. Notice what makes a man a dad:

• **The Character That He Lives**

The Bible says, "Blessed is every one that feareth the LORD; that walketh in his ways" (Psalm 128:1).

Character is what we are in the dark when no one is looking. D. L. Moody said, "Our children do as we say until they are fifteen, and then they do as we do."

A little boy was being driven to school by his mother when he asked, "Why is it the idiots only come out when Dad takes me to school?" Actions are louder than words!

Did you know that when a father is an active believer in Christ there is a 75 percent likelihood that his children will also become active believers? But if only the mother is a believer, the likelihood is drastically reduced to 15 percent. Fathers have a tremendous responsibility to model character.

• The Care That He Lends

The Bible says, "For thou shalt eat the labour of thine hands . . ." (Psalm 128:2). The text is talking about a dad working and providing for his family.

Someone has observed that children go through four stages in their communication with their fathers. First, they call us "Da-Da." Then they call us "Daddy." Next they call us "Dad." Finally, they call us collect.

Women and children, if you are blessed with a husband and a father who provides for the family, thank him on a regular basis.

I also would like to remind the fathers of America – even if you have divorced your child's mother – you still have a moral obligation to provide for the child. (1 Timothy 5:8) If you are a deadbeat dad, get up off your duff, get a job, and support your family! It is not the government's responsibility to support your family. It is yours!

• The Companion That He Loves

"Thy wife shall be as a fruitful vine by the sides of thine house . . ." (Psalm 128:3). Notice I said companion, not companions. The Bible speaks of fruitful vine, not fruitful vines. Yes, the Bible talks of one woman and one man for a lifetime.

I am convinced the greatest thing I can do for my daughter Savannah is to love her mother. It was interesting for me to learn that daughters many times marry men like their fathers. (This explains why mothers cry at weddings!) Fathers, if you want your daughter's husband to be loving, you had better be loving to your wife. Let your children see you embracing your wife, holding her hand, and expressing the love you have for her. The greatest leadership principle I have ever learned is "monkey see, monkey do."

• The Children That He Leads

The Bible says, ". . . thy children like olive plants round about thy table" (Psalm 128:3).

It was interesting to learn that in order for olive plants to survive they must be cultivated. Allow me to share with you six ways in which a father cultivates his children:

1. Spend time with your children.

Did you know the average father in America communicates 48 seconds a day with his children? Yes, if the devil can't make us bad, he will make us busy.

Jim Bakker, former PTL founder, spoke at a Pastor's Conference in Phoenix, Arizona. He said while he was in prison his son came to visit. Mr. Bakker said as his son was leaving this is what he said. " 'Dad,' he told me as he embraced me and said goodbye, 'this has been the greatest day of my whole life. All I ever wanted is to have you all to myself for one whole day. Today was like a dream come true for me!'" Mr. Bakker said, "Men, do not win the world and lose your own sons and daughters!"

I did not meet my father until I was thirty years of age. The only gift he ever gave me was a very nice watch. I put it on every Father's Day and think of him. It is an expensive watch; but I assure you I would gladly trade it to have had a day on the lake or a day at the park or a round on the golf course with my dad. Dads, presents never replace your presence. Spend time with your children!

2. Give your children spiritual training.

I encourage you to pray with your children, take them to church, and see that they are involved in Sunday school, Vacation Bible School, and church camp. One of the things my wife and I do to assist the spiritual training of our daughter is we give her an allowance for every Christian book she reads. We decided that if we wanted to raise a garbage man we would pay our child for taking out the trash. If you want your children to be great men or women of God, pay them to read good books.

3. Discipline your children.

A recent poll revealed that 90 percent of graduating high school seniors wished their parents and teachers had loved them enough to discipline them more. I am convinced children want rules but they want them with relationships. It is rules without relationships that lead to rebellion.

To say your children do not need discipline is to say you are doing a better job than God in your parenting. Yes, even God has to discipline His children. (Hebrews 12:8)

I always remind myself when I discipline Savannah (and I assure you it hurts; she's a daddy's girl) that I am not doing something to her but for her. If I love her like I should, I must discipline her.

4. Teach them the work ethic.

I am convinced we are raising scores of lazy children. One young lady, trying to be a little hip, walked up to her dad and said, "Dad, can I have some mun to hit the flick?" (Translation: "Dad, can I have some money to go to the movies?") He looked at her and said, "No, you can't have some mun to go to the flick. But you can swish the dish, spread the bed, and flop the mop!"

Children need chores and responsibilities. I was raised by a stepfather who only required that I work a half-day. I could choose whichever twelve hours I wanted. Teach your children to work because nothing will work in their lives until they do.

5. Teach them respect.

I am talking about respecting other people and other people's property and possessions. Several years ago my mother came to our church for Homecoming.

We had what I thought was an awesome day. We had a great service, a wonderful crowd, and a delicious meal. But after it was over, my mother asked if she could speak with me. She said, "I thought I taught you respect." I immediately asked what she was referring to. She said, "The nerve of you to allow the young people to eat before the senior citizens. Son, should we not pay honor to our elders?" She was correct, I assure you. Now our seniors are at the front of the line at every meal we have at our church. You never know how far the impact of respecting someone may reach.

A New York businessman dropped a dollar into the cup of a man selling pencils and hurriedly stepped aboard the subway train. On second thought, he stepped back off the train, walked over to the beggar, and took several pencils from him. Apologetically, he explained that in his haste he had neglected to pick up his pencils and hoped the man would not be upset with him. "After all," he said, "you are a businessman just like me. You have merchandise to sell, and it's fairly priced." Then he caught the next train.

At a social function a few months later, a neatly dressed salesman stepped up to the businessman and introduced himself. "You probably don't remember me, and I don't know your name; but I will never forget you. You are the man who gave me back my self-respect. I was a 'beggar' selling pencils until you came along and told me I was a businessman." Let's teach our children to respect themselves and others.

6. Teach them money management.

Most of us know what Proverbs 22:6 says: "Train up a child in the way he should go: and when he is old, he will not depart from it." But did you ever notice the following verses? "The rich ruleth over the poor, and the borrower is servant to the lender" (Proverbs 22:7). We are to teach them money management and the value of a dollar.

One reason parents cannot teach their children the principle of money management is because they have never learned it themselves.

Today most people can be divided into three groups:

• The haves.
• The have-nots.
• The have-not-paid-for what they have.

We buy the things we don't need with the money we don't have to impress people we don't like. I often see bumper stickers that read: "I owe, I owe, so off to work I go!" I have a feeling that the message is more serious than it is funny.

I am reminded of a handyman who had been called out to a millionaire's mansion to refinish her floors. The woman of the house said, "Be especially careful of this dining room table. It goes back to Louis XIV." The handyman said, "Lady, don't feel bad. If I don't make a payment by Friday, my whole dining room suite goes back to Rich's the sixteenth!"

I encourage the people of my congregation to quit trying to keep up with the Joneses. Even if you do catch them, they will just refinance. A great plan for teaching money management is to teach children to give 10 percent, save 10 percent, and spend the other 80 percent wisely. Teach your children to manage money; or I assure you, money will manage them.

• The Contributions That He Leaves

Notice Psalm 128:4-6: "Behold, that thus shall the man be blessed that feareth the LORD. The LORD shall bless thee out of Zion: and thou shalt see the good of Jerusalem all the days of thy life. Yea, thou shalt see thy children's children, and peace upon Israel."

Isn't it encouraging to know we have the opportunity to make a spiritual impact on our children and grandchildren? We cannot do anything about our ancestors, but we can do something about our descendants.

Yes, the godly father leaves a godly legacy; and this is far more important than an inheritance. An inheritance is something you leave *for* your children, and a legacy is something you leave *in* them.

D. L. Moody said, "If you want to know what kind of father you are, don't look at your children; look at your grandchildren."

I keep a picture of my daughter Savannah Abigail in my Bible in Proverbs chapter 20. I intentionally want it there because the seventh verse says, "The just man walketh in his integrity: his children are blessed after him." I want that constant reminder that I need to stay close and clean. If I should fail, my children, grandchildren, and great-grandchildren will be negatively effected. But if I walk with God, they will be blessed. The following story illustrates this principle extremely well.

Max Jukes lived in New York. He did not believe in Christ or in Christian training. He refused to take his children to church – even when they asked to go. He has had 1,026 descendants: 300 were sent to prison for an average term of thirteen years; 190 were prostitutes; 680 were admitted alcoholics. His family, thus far, has cost the state in excess of $420,000. They made no contribution to society.

Evangelist Jonathan Edwards lived in the same state at the same time as Jukes. He loved the Lord and saw that his children were in church every Sunday – as he served the Lord to the best of his ability. Of his 929 descendants, 430 were ministers; eighty-six became professors; thirteen became university presidents; seventy-five authored great books; and seven were elected to the United States Congress. One was vice president of his nation. Jonathan Edwards' family never cost the state one cent but has contributed immeasurably to the life of plenty in this land today.

I realize we live in a success-driven world. Men want to rise to the top at any cost. I believe many times though we are like monkeys. The higher we climb, the more we show our tails. I think the following poem gives us a definition of real success:

You can use most any measure
When you are speaking of success.

You can measure it in lovely homes,
Expensive cars, or dress;

But the measure of your real success
Is one you cannot spend.

It is the way your child describes you
When he is talking to his friend.

CHAPTER EIGHT

The Top Ten Marriage Killers

A small rural church was having service one day when the devil himself walked in the front door and came down the aisle of the church. The people went hysterical, jumping through the windows and running for the doors. After the commotion ceased, one man was still nonchalantly seated in his pew. The devil approached him and asked, "Aren't you scared of me?" The man firmly replied, "Not in the least." The devil asked, "Why not?" The man said, "I have been married to your sister for thirty years!"

I recently read some startling facts. Five out of every ten marriages end in divorce. Another 10 percent separate and stay separated. This tells me six out of every ten marriages are going bad. Do you know what happens with the four who stay together? Two stay together for the children or other reasons; and the other two experience a happy, fulfilled relationship. Every twenty-seven seconds in America, there is a divorce. That is more than 7,000 a day! Allow me to share with you ten killers of marriages in America:

1. Physical fatigue

The disciples of the Lord were one time so busy doing ministry that they even neglected time to eat and rest. And Jesus said to them, "Come ye yourselves apart into a desert place, and rest a while" (Mark 6:31). Sometimes if we don't go apart, we will come apart.

The truth is many marriages are coming apart because of fatigue. We are busy raising children, going to school, building for the future, building a house and a career that we are too tired as a couple to really enjoy each other. When we become that tired, we are too tired! If the devil can't make us bad, he will make us too busy.

I constantly battle this issue because I am a workaholic by nature. It is extremely easy for me to get so caught up with doing good things that I miss out on the best things. I encourage you to start saying "no" to the *good* things, so you can say "yes" to the *best* things.

Dr. Johnny Hunt has a great threefold plan for maintaining his relationship with his wife:

A. **Dialogue daily.** Take time for conversation every day.

B. **Date weekly.** Barbara and I usually date one night a week. Sometimes we just go to dinner and come home and watch a movie. I assure you every Monday we have lunch together. A weekly date is very important!

C. **Depart quarterly.** Yes, it is great to get away from all the disturbances and just be together. I have discovered that I must take time to be holy, but I also must take time to be a hubby.

2. Financial conflicts

Have you and your mate had an argument over finances? Today? Financial counselor Larry Burkett says credit is the motivating factor behind 80 percent of all divorces. I realize debt is not always bad and we are all in debt. When we came into this world, we owed our mothers for nine months of room and board. But debt can lead to problems because money problems do cause marriage problems.

Debt is wrong:

• when it is beyond your ability to repay it on time.

• when it prevents you from giving to God what is right.

• when the burden is so heavy you cannot save for the future.

• if it puts your family under financial pressure.

• if it is used to pay for the luxuries of life.

As a rule of thumb, keep this in mind: it is all right to borrow for necessities, but you should pay cash for luxuries. So, if at all possible, pay cash or don't buy it.

I have learned these six lessons about finances:

• **Make large purchases slowly.**

The problem with young couples is they want in four years what it took Mom and Dad forty years to accomplish.

• **Make purchases in agreement.**

I would never make a large purchase without Barbara's consent. I was born at night but not last night.

• **Separate your needs and greeds.**

Remember that God promised to supply your needs, not greeds. (Philippians 4:19)

• **Realize happiness is not in things.**

• **Perform plastic surgery on your charge cards.**

• **Give God the first 10 percent of your income.**

3. Selfishness

A lady said to her pastor, "My husband is the most selfish man in the world." The pastor said, "Why do you say that?" She said, "He won a trip to Hawaii for two, and he went twice!"

The Bible says, "Let nothing be done through strife or vainglory; but in lowliness of mind let each esteem other better than themselves" (Philippians 2:3).

I once worked with a man who every time his wife purchased a new blouse he had to have a new shirt. How selfish! By the way, he is now divorced.

There is only one way to overcome selfishness. It is through giving. The Bible says to submit yourselves "one to another in the fear of God" (Ephesians 5:21). That means we are to put our mate's interest before our own. This can be done only through a proper relationship with God.

4. Immaturity

The Bible says, "When I was a child, I spake as a child, I understood as a child, I thought as a child: but when I became a man, I put away childish things" (1 Corinthians 13:11). The truth is that people are only young once, but they can be immature for a lifetime.

One man told his marriage counselor, "My wife is so immature. I can be taking a bath, and she will come in and sink my boats." The bottom line is *many people need to grow up.*

I have often been asked, "Pastor, do you and your wife ever argue?" I respond, "No, but we do sometimes have intense fellowship." We purposed when we first got married to never go to bed upset at each other. And after almost twenty years of marriage, we have not; but we have stayed up for two or three days at a time.

My wife and I spent many years disagreeing about our in-laws. I would not give an inch and neither would she. It was a great day when we started practicing what the Scripture teaches in this area: "But avoid foolish questions, and genealogies, and contentions . . ." (Titus 3:9). We agreed neither of us would speak negatively about the other's family. We decided to grow up a little. The bottom line is if she is a Democrat and you are a Republican don't talk politics.

If you happen to be an in-law, let me share with you a four-step plan for being an asset and not a liability in your child's marriage:

- Hands off.
- Prayers on.
- Mouths closed.
- Hearts open.

5. Pride

Mark Twain said, "Temper gets you in trouble, but pride keeps you there." I am amazed at the number of couples that are more concerned with who is right than what is right.

I was once in a counseling session in which a lady told me after several years of marriage her husband had never apologized to her. Get real! Does anybody think they are that good? Two magical words in any relationship are: "I'm sorry." If you want to stay married, you will learn to say them often.

6. Pettiness

The Song of Solomon is an awesome book. It deals with the relationship of Solomon and his bride. It was interesting to me that Solomon said it is "the little foxes" that "spoil the vines" (2:15). Solomon knew it was the small things that many times destroy the relationship.

"He leaves the toothpaste top off." "She doesn't cook dressing like my mother." We can allow little issues to cause major problems.

A couple was celebrating their golden wedding anniversary when a young lady asked the wife what she attributed to fifty years of marriage. Her response was interesting to say the least. "Before we married, I decided to overlook his top ten faults. I never wrote out a list. Although every time he messed up, I would just say to myself, 'Luckily for you, that's on the list.' " Learn to overlook the small stuff!

7. Unrealistic expectations

Because I am a denominational leader, I have many churches contact me when they are searching for pastoral candidates. Sometimes the qualifications they set amaze me. To be honest, many times they are unrealistic. But it is encouraging to know after hundreds of years the perfect pastor has been found! See below:

He is the pastor who will please everyone. He preaches exactly twenty minutes and then sits down. He condemns sin but never steps on anybody's toes.

He works from eight in the morning to ten at night, doing everything from preaching sermons to sweeping. He makes $400 per week, gives $100 a week to the church, drives a late-model car, buys lots of books, wears fine clothes, and has a nice family. He always stands ready to contribute to every other cause, too, and help panhandlers who drop by the church on their way to somewhere.

He is thirty-six years old and has been preaching forty years. He is tall, on the short side; heavyset, in a thin sort of way; and handsome. He has eyes of blue and brown (to fit the occasion) and wears his hair parted in the middle: left side, dark and straight; right side, brown and wavy.

He has a burning desire to work with the youth and spends all his time with the senior citizens. He smiles all the time while keeping a straight face because he has a keen sense of humor that finds him seriously dedicated. He makes fifteen calls a day on church members, spends all his time evangelizing nonmembers, and is always found in his study if he is needed. Unfortunately, he burnt himself out and died at the age of thirty-two.

Unrealistic expectations also will kill a marriage relationship. At church, we sing "In the Sweet By and By"; but the reality is that we are living in the nasty now and now. It is not how we think it ought to be but how it is that really counts. Unrealistic expectations in any relationship will destroy it. I have seen many times in a marriage relationship what one thinks he is getting and what he/she actually gets are greatly different.

The Ideal Wife: What Every Man Expects

Always beautiful and cheerful. Could have married a movie star but wanted only you. Hair that never needs curlers or beauty shops.

Beauty that won't run in a rainstorm. Never sick—just allergic to jewelry and fur coats.

Insists that moving furniture by herself is good for her figure.

Expert in cooking, cleaning house, fixing the car or TV, painting the house, and keeping quiet.

Favorite hobbies: mowing the lawn and shoveling snow.

Hates charge cards.

Her favorite expression: "What can I do for you, dear?"

Thinks you have Einstein's brain but look like Mr. Universe.

Wishes you would go out with the boys, so she could get some sewing done.

Loves you because you are sexy.

What He Gets:

She speaks 140 words a minute with gusts up to 180.

She was once a model for a totem pole.

A light eater: as soon as it gets light, she starts eating.

Where there's smoke, there she is – cooking.

She lets you know you only have two faults: everything you say and everything you do.

No matter what she does with it, her hair looks like an explosion in a steel wool factory.

The Ideal Husband: What Every Woman Expects

He will be a brilliant conversationalist.

A very sensitive man, kind and understanding, truly loving.

A very hard-working man.

A man who helps around the house by washing dishes, vacuuming floors, and taking care of the yard.

Someone who helps his wife raise the children.

A man of emotional and physical strength.

A man who is as smart as Einstein but looks like a younger Robert Redford.

What She Gets:

He always takes her to the best restaurants. Some day he may even take her inside.

He doesn't have any ulcers; he gives them.

Anytime he has an idea in his head, he has the whole thing in a nutshell.

He's a well-known miracle worker; it's a miracle when he works.

He supports his wife in the manner to which she was accustomed; he's letting her keep her job.

He's such a bore that he even bores his wife when he gives her a compliment.

He has occasional flashes of silence that make his conversation brilliant.

8. Lack of intimacy

Years ago, I read a great book, *His Needs, Her Needs,* by Willard Harley. In it, he addresses the top five needs of men and women. It was interesting that a man's number-one need was sexual fulfillment and a woman's was affection. This teaches me that intimacy is vital to the husband-and-wife relationship.

The Bible also teaches that we are to meet each other's needs in this area: "Nevertheless, to avoid fornication, let every man have his own wife, and let every woman have her own husband. Let the husband render unto the wife due benevolence: and likewise also the wife unto the husband. The wife hath not power of her own body, but the husband: and likewise also the husband hath not power of his own body, but the wife" (1 Corinthians 7:2-5).

A man went to the doctor because of severe depression; and after a little while, the doctor asked him to go out into the waiting area and send in his wife. Once the wife came in, the doctor shared what the man needed in order to recover. "He needs a delicious breakfast with a kiss before sending him off to work each day. Then when he comes home for lunch, give him a gentle massage. When he comes home from work, have a candlelight dinner for him and see that his needs are met every night he wishes." After hearing the doctor, she went to the waiting area to meet her husband. He asked, "What did the doctor say?" She blurted out, "He said you're going to die!" Intimacy is vital!

9. Jealousy

Solomon acknowledged the devastation of jealousy when he said it is "cruel as the grave" (Song of Solomon 8:6). It will destroy relationships. It caused Cain to murder Abel, Esau to hate Jacob, and the elder brother to resent the prodigal.

I realize past history can produce a propensity to acts of jealousy, but many times it stems from poor self-image of the one that is jealous. Yes, they feel they really don't deserve the person they have; and they constantly fear losing him or her to someone who does. The issue is not jealousy but low self-esteem. The solution is building the individual's self-esteem.

A gentleman was in a department store when he saw a very attractive young lady and asked her if she would talk to him. He said, "The problem is I have lost my wife in here; and usually if I speak to a beautiful woman, she appears out of nowhere." Jealousy is a marriage killer.

10. Spiritual Disobedience

I still do believe a family that prays together stays together; and when we go against God's grain, we will get splinters. I recently ran across some intriguing American stats. Check these out:

- One out of every two marriages ends in divorce.

- One out of every fifty marriages ends in a divorce if the couple had a church wedding.

- One out of 105 marriages ends in divorce if the couple attends church on a regular basis.

- One out of 1,005 marriages ends in a divorce if the couple attends church on a regular basis and has family prayer time together.

It is very obvious that spiritual obedience does make a difference.

A little boy went to the pet store to buy a puppy. There were lots of puppies, but one was sitting over in the corner wagging his tail. The little fellow noticed this particular puppy and said, "I want the one with the happy ending."

That is what I desire with all of my heart. I hope for Barbara and me to be able to spend our last days on earth together. Maybe we'll be rocking in Cracker Barrel rocking chairs somewhere. If she can say to me, "The greatest decision I ever made – other than accepting Christ – was marrying you," I will have had a happy ending. I surely hope you have one too!

CHAPTER NINE

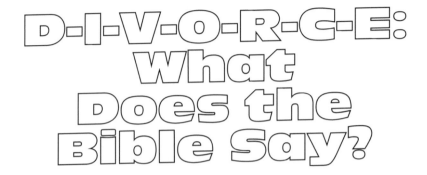

Matthew 19:1-14

1. And it came to pass, that when Jesus had finished these sayings, he departed from Galilee, and came into the coasts of Judaea beyond Jordan;

2. And great multitudes followed him; and he healed them there.

3. The Pharisees also came unto him, tempting him, and saying unto him, Is it lawful for a man to put away his wife for every cause?

4. And he answered and said unto them, Have ye not read, that he which made them at the beginning made them male and female,

5. And said, For this cause shall a man leave father and mother, and shall cleave to his wife: and they twain shall be one flesh?

6. Wherefore they are no more twain, but one flesh. What there-

fore God hath joined together, let not man put asunder.

7. They say unto him, Why did Moses then command to give a writing of divorcement, and to put her away?

8. He saith unto them, Moses because of the hardness of your hearts suffered you to put away your wives: but from the beginning it was not so.

9. And I say unto you, Whosoever shall put away his wife, except it be for fornication, and shall marry another, committeth adultery: and whose marrieth her which is put away doth commit adultery.

10. His disciples say unto him, If the case of the man be so with his wife, it is not good to marry.

11. But he said unto them, All men cannot receive this saying, save they to whom it is given.

12. For there are some eunuchs, which were so born from their mother's womb: and there are some eunuchs, which were made eunuchs of men: and there be eunuchs, which have made themselves eunuchs for the kingdom of heaven's sake. He that is able to receive it, let him receive it.

13. Then were there brought unto him little children, that he should put his hands on them, and pray: and the disciples rebuked them.

14. But Jesus said, Suffer little children, and forbid them not, to come unto me: for of such is the kingdom of heaven.

The average American has a nonchalant attitude when it comes to the subject of divorce. A divorce center in California recently had on their marquee:

"Divorce: $25. Unload That Turkey." What a flippant attitude! If you don't believe America has a flippant attitude toward divorce, just turn on your TV. Watch "As Your Stomach Turns" or one of the many daily kangaroo courts in America, and what do you see? You see people in and out of relationship after relationship.

Did you know that in America there is a divorce every twenty-seven seconds? That is 7,000 a day! It is amazing that 50 percent of first-time marriages end in divorce; 65 percent of second marriages end in divorce; 75 percent is the divorce rate of second-timers if children are involved; and 75 percent of third-time marriages end in divorce. What is even more amazing to me is that 45 percent say they expect it to end in divorce even before they marry. "If it doesn't work out, I'll just get a divorce and marry someone else," they will say. The problem is this: it is easier to get a marriage license than a driver's license!

Even though society has this lackadaisical attitude, I can't get away from what the Bible teaches. "Therefore shall a man leave his father and his mother, and shall cleave unto his wife: and they shall be one flesh" (Genesis 2:24).

The perfect plan of God is one man for one woman for one lifetime. We must understand that God hates divorce. (Malachi 2:16) Notice: I did not say He hates divorcees. He hates murder, but He loves the murderer. He hates sin but loves the sinner. He hates divorce because of the spiritual, physical, emotional, mental, and financial pain it brings to people.

Divorce greatly affects the two individuals in the marriage. Experts tell us the emotional pain will last half the time of the marriage. If a twenty-year marriage ends, they say the emotional pain will exist at least ten more years. I personally know of couples who never have gotten past the emotional pain of a divorce.

There is also the financial pain. The average divorce cost in America is $16,000. In every divorce, there are four people legally involved. There are two winners (the attorneys) and two losers (the divorcees). Did you know the standard of living declines for 73 percent of women and children after a divorce? Did you know only 14 percent of all divorce settlements include alimony and only 2 percent of divorced mothers receive more than $5,000 a year from their ex-husbands?

Sadly, husbands and wives are certainly not the only ones affected by divorce. Interestingly, in both of the Gospels after Jesus addressed divorce, He spoke of children. (Matthew 19:13-15 and Mark 10:13-16) Jesus knew children would be tremendously affected. Every twenty-four hours, 3,000 children see their parents divorce and their lives greatly impacted.

Please note six of the many ways divorce impacts children:

1. Self-blame

They say things like: "If I had been a boy or if I had been a girl, this would not be happening." "If I had behaved better . . ." "It is my fault." Children blame themselves for the divorce.

2. Lack of Love

In America, 50 percent of divorced children have not seen their father in a year.

3. Resentment

Many times when they see a happy family, they resent it and wonder why it can not be that way with their mother and father.

4. Insecurity

Their security has been shattered, and they live in fear of losing the other security they possess.

5. Bitterness

This attitude may be toward one or both parents.

6. Self-esteem

They feel they simply are not as good as others because their parents are not together.

Below are three guidelines for children of divorced parents:

1. **Don't blame yourself.** It is *not* your fault!

2. **Respect your parents' decision.** You probably don't know all the facts. They are your parents, and they deserve your respect.

3. **Refuse to be an informant for either of your parents.**

The bottom line is that parents should exhaust all measures to keep their family together! There are two things you do not want to do prematurely. One is to resort to divorce; the other is to embalm a body.

The Pharisees asked Jesus, "Is it lawful to get a divorce?" (Matthew 19:3) Keep in mind they asked John the Baptist the very same question, and his answer cost him his head. (Matthew 14:4, 10) I love how Jesus responded: "Have ye not read . . . ?" (Matthew 19:4). He took them to the Word of God, and that is where we need to go today when we deal with the issue. He shared, "Moses because of the hardness of your hearts suffered you to put away your wives . . ." (Matthew 19:8). Moses did allow for divorce because of the ill treatment the Hebrew women were receiving from their husbands (their lives were at risk) and to stop polygamy. But please notice the latter part of the verse: "but from the beginning it was not so." Again, God's perfect plan is one man for one woman for one lifetime.

Are there biblical grounds for divorce and remarriage? Certainly, and the Bible teaches us what they are. In order to really understand what Christ teaches, it is important to understand what was being taught about divorce during that time.

There were two prominent rabbis, Hillel and Shammai, who were teaching greatly contrasting views of divorce. Rabbi Hillel said you could divorce your wife for burning dinner, putting too much salt in your food, talking to another man, or if you found someone prettier. You could divorce for almost anything. Rabbi Shammai said there were no grounds for divorce. The people were as confused as a termite in a yo-yo. Jesus heard their questions and shared biblical grounds for divorce and remarriage.

My thoughts are defined below:

1. Adultery

Jesus said, "Whosoever shall put away his wife, except it be for fornication, and shall marry another, committeth adultery . . ." (Matthew 19:9). "Fornication" comes from the Greek work *pornia* from which we get the word "pornography" which means sexual immorality.

I have often been asked as a pastor if I believe in the exception clause for divorce. I always answer, "I sure do. If Jesus did, I certainly do too." Please understand the Bible does permit for divorce where *adultery* is involved. It does not command divorce, but God does allow for it. I truly believe the perfect plan of God is for a couple to stay together – even after an affair has taken place. However, God does permit divorce under this circumstance because sometimes reconciliation is not possible.

2. A Death-to-Life Experience

The Bible says, "We know that we have passed from death unto life, because we love the brethren . . ." (1 John 3:14). This Scripture is compared with a salvation experience. It discusses the transformation that takes place when a person receives Jesus Christ.

Let's suppose that before a person received Christ he/she went through a divorce (or multiple divorces) then received Christ as their Savior. I am glad to report to you that God forgave all their sin! The Bible says, "If we confess our sins, he is faithful and just to forgive us our sins, and to cleanse us from all unrighteousness" (1 John 1:9).

I once did an indepth study on the word "all." And it means all, entirely, everything! Yes, when a person receives Christ, He forgives them of murder, robbery, homosexuality, and even divorce. That person is free to remarry without condemnation.

3. **Desertion by an unbeliever** (1 Corinthians 7:13-15)

13. And the woman which hath an husband that believeth not, and if he be pleased to dwell with her, let her not leave him.

14. For the unbelieving husband is sanctified by the wife, and the unbelieving wife is sanctified by the husband: else were your children unclean; but now are they holy.

15. But if the unbelieving depart, let him depart. A brother or a sister is not under bondage in such cases: but God hath called us to peace.

The Bible here is very clear that if a believer is married to an unbeliever the believer is to stay in the marriage in hopes of reaching the unbeliever for Christ. But if the unbeliever leaves the believer, the believer is free and not under bondage. Desertion is biblical grounds for divorce.

I am asked often: "What about irreconcilable differences?" "What about this situation or that?" I have given you the biblical grounds for divorce and remarriage.

A lady once said to me: "Pastor, I am in my second marriage; and I did not have biblical grounds for divorce. What should I do? Go back to my first husband?" I then shared with her what I believe to be the biblical answer. First, you should not go back to your first husband. That would be a violation of

Scripture. See Deuteronomy 24:1-4 below:

1. When a man hath taken a wife, and married her, and it come to pass that she find no favour in his eyes, because he hath found some uncleanness in her: than let him write her a bill of divorcement, and give *it* in her hand, and send her out of his house.

2. And when she is departed out of his house, she may go and be another man's *wife.*

3. And *if* the latter husband hate her, and write her a bill of divorcement, and giveth *it* in her hand, and sendeth her out of his house; or if the latter husband die, which took her *to be* his wife;

4. Her former husband, which sent her away, may not take her again to be his wife, after that she is defiled; for that is abomination before the LORD: and thou shalt not cause the land to sin, which the LORD thy God giveth thee *for* an inheritance.

You can't unscramble an egg! I then shared with her to ask God for forgiveness and move on with her life. I learned years ago that we can reflect on the scars or reach for the stars. *God forgives!*

It was extremely encouraging to me when I realized that anything I can remember God can forget. Scores of divorcees need to accept the forgiveness of God and move on.

I am asked, "What should the stand of the church be concerning divorce?" I relate it to two people standing on top of the cliff contemplating jumping. I want to be there with them, begging them: "Please don't do it!" But I also assure you if they do I want to have an ambulance at the bottom ready to take them to the hospital. The church's attitude should be if we can not save the marriage, we at least want to save the people. It is a sad reproach on the church when divorced people find more love, concern, and acceptance at the singles bar than they do at the church. Maybe that's why more divorcees are at the singles bar than at the church! For too long, the church has made divorcees feel like second-class citizens. I say to every divorced person: "God has a great plan for your life!" What the devil meant for bad, God can use for good.

One of my favorite Bible stories is found in John 8:1-11:

1. Jesus went unto the mount of Olives.

2. And early in the morning he came again into the temple, and all the people came unto him; and he sat down, and taught them.

3. And the scribes and Pharisees brought unto him a woman taken in adultery; and when they had set her in the midst,

4. They say unto him, Master, this woman was taken in adultery, in the very act.

5. Now Moses in the law commanded us, that such should be stoned: but what sayest thou?

6. This they said, tempting him, that they might have to accuse him. But Jesus stooped down, and with his finger wrote on the ground, as though he heard them not.

7. So when they continued asking him, he lifted up himself, and said unto them, He that is without sin among you, let him first cast a stone at her.

8. And again he stooped down, and wrote on the ground.

9. And they which heard it, being convicted by *their own* conscience, went out one by one, beginning at the eldest, *even* unto

the last: and Jesus was left alone, and the woman standing in the midst.

10. When Jesus had lifted up himself, and saw none but the woman, he said unto her, Woman, where are those thine accusers? hath no man condemned thee?

11. She said, No man, Lord. And Jesus said unto her, Neither do I condemn thee: go, and sin no more.

The Pharisees (the religious sect of the day) brought a woman to Jesus and said, "We caught her committing adultery – in the very act, and the law says she should be stoned." They knew part of the law – the part they agreed with, but the law *also said* the man should be stoned. (Leviticus 20:10) Wonder why they didn't bring him? Was he one of their buddies? The Bible says when Jesus heard them He just wrote on the ground. Do you ever wonder what He wrote? I don't know; but I think He might have written May 12, August 8, November 15 – the days they had been to her house. He looked at them and said, "He that is without sin among you, let him first cast a stone at her." Upon hearing this, the text says they, like being convicted, began to put down their stones and walk away – the eldest first down to the youngest. I have often thought the eldest left first because he probably had been to her house most often.

I like what my black preacher friend said. He shared if they had cast those stones Jesus would have turned them to rubber and they would have bounced back, knocking the accusers' brains out.

I also like what Jesus said after they all left: "Woman, where are those thine accusers? hath no man condemned thee? . . . Neither do I condemn thee: go, and sin no more." It thrills my heart to know Jesus did not come to rub our sin in but to RUB IT OUT!

CHAPTER TEN

The foundation for this chapter is a statement I heard Dr. James Dobson make: "Today we are so busy giving our children what we didn't have, we are not giving them what we did have." I do not believe there has ever been a truer statement.

I recently read the five most popular traits parents in America want their children to possess:

1. Responsibility.
2. Good manners.
3. Tolerant.
4. Faith.
5. Independent.

My wife Barbara and I discussed these traits and made a list of the qualities we want our daughter to possess:

- To love and obey God. (Matthew 22:37) Notice, not only to love God but also to obey Him.

- To possess a good self-image. The Bible says, "Thou shalt love thy neighbour as thyself" (Matthew 22:39). We can not love others like we should until we first love ourselves.

- To take responsibility for her life. We do not want her to play the blame game.

- To have a good mental attitude. The Bible says that as a man "thinketh in his heart, so is he" (Proverbs 23:7).

- To show a thankful spirit. The Bible says, "In every thing give thanks . . ." (1 Thessalonians 5:18). Notice, not *for* everything but *in* everything. I learned a long time ago that:

> *from the day of your birth*
> *until your ride in the hearse*
> *things are never so bad*
> *that they couldn't be worse.*

An attitude of gratitude is crucial.

I am convinced in order for us to foster proper qualities in our children we must give them some things. Allow me to share with you seven ways the Bible teaches us to encourage them:

1. **Love.**

I am talking about unconditional love. A wonderful example is found in Luke 15. A son asked his father for his inheritance and went out and started living a very sinful life. He digressed so low he eventually ended up in the pig pen. But when the day came that he got his belly full of the swine's husks, he decided things were far better at home and he would like to go back there. He wondered if his father would take him back. As he journeyed toward home, guess who was waiting and watching for him? You guessed it. His father! When the father saw him, he ran toward his son and began to hug and kiss him. He said, "Let's have a party." Notice, his father did not rebuke him for his past actions but rather provided him with unconditional love. This story is symbolic of God our Heavenly Father and the unconditional love He has for us.

God wants us to follow His example by loving our children with an unconditional love. The answer to many of the problems our children are facing is unconditional love. Could the answer to drugs be hugs?

Charles Swindoll said, "Many a young woman who opts for immoral sexual relationships does so because she can scarcely remember a time when her father so much as touched her. Unaffectionate dads, without wishing to do so, can trigger a daughter's promiscuity." Unconditional love provides two essentials for our children:

A. **Intimacy.** Unconditional love will bond you with your children. Aren't we all looking for people who will love us unconditionally? Don't you have more intimate relationships with those who love you in this way?

B. **Security.** Experts agree the greatest things parents can do to combat the peer pressure their children face is to provide security at home. Yes, I believe children can face rejection at every other place as long as they know they have unconditional love and security at home. This security also gives them the ability to take risks with the freedom to fail.

Olympic gymnast Cathy Rigby was the hope of the United States in Munich, Germany. She had one goal in mind: excellence! Before the games began, she prayed for the strength to move through the routine without making a mistake. She performed well, but she did not win. Emotionally, she was crushed. She joined her parents in the stands – ready for a good cry. "I'm sorry," she said, "I did my best." Today Cathy recalls ten words from her mother that she will never forget: "Doing your best is more important than being the best." Unconditional love really does build security!

2. Lift them.

David purposed in his heart that he would praise his son daily. (Psalm 72:15) All people respond to praises and raises. We need to give our children more strokes than pokes. Children want praise! A little boy said to his father, "Daddy, let's play darts. I'll throw, and you say wonderful."

Too many parents' method of parenting is to observe their children doing something wrong and reprimanding them. Why don't we watch for them to do something right and reward them? I assure you for every one wrong thing they do they will do ten things right.

Also, when you reward your child, focus on character more than achievement. Every child cannot make the honor roll, win the beauty contest, make the all-star team, or be musically inclined; but every child can be thankful, obedient, polite, and work hard.

A Yale University president some years ago gave this advice to a former president of Ohio State: "Always be kind to your A and B students. Someday one of them will return to your campus as a good professor. Also be kind to your C students. Someday one of them will return and build you a 2-million-dollar science laboratory." Reward character more than achievement!

A teacher in New York decided to honor each of the seniors in her high school by telling them the difference each one had made. Using a process developed by Helice Bridges of Del Mar, California, she called each student to the front of the class – one at a time. First, she told them how the student made a difference to her and the class. Then she presented each of them with a blue ribbon imprinted with gold letters that read: "Who I Am Makes a Difference."

Afterwards, the teacher decided to do a class project to see what kind of impact recognition would have on the community. She gave each of the students three more ribbons and instructed them to go out and spread this acknowledgement ceremony. Then they were to follow up on the results, see who honored whom, and report back to the class in about a week.

One of the boys in the class went to a junior executive in a nearby company and honored him for helping him with his career planning. He gave him a blue ribbon and put it on his shirt. Then he gave him two extra ribbons and said, "We're doing a class project on recognition; and we'd like you to go out, find somebody to honor, give him a blue ribbon, then give him the extra blue ribbon; so he can acknowledge a third person to keep this acknowledgement ceremony going. Then please report back to me and tell me what happened."

Later that day the junior executive went in to see his boss who had been noted, by the way, as being a kind of grouchy fellow. He sat his boss down and told him he deeply admired him for being a creative genius. The boss seemed very surprised. The junior executive asked him if he would accept the gift of the blue ribbon and would give him permission to put it on him. His surprised boss said, "Well, sure."

The junior executive took the blue ribbon and placed it on his boss's jacket above his heart. As he gave him the last ribbon, he said, "Would you do me a favor? Would you take this extra ribbon and pass it on by honoring someone else? The young boy who first gave me the ribbons is doing a project in school, and we want to keep this recognition ceremony going and find out how it affects people."

That night the boss came home to his fourteen-year-old son and sat him down. He said, "The most incredible thing happened to me today. I was in my office, and one of the junior executives came in and told me that he admired me and gave me a blue ribbon for being a creative genius. Imagine! He thinks I'm a creative genius! Then he put this blue ribbon that says, 'Who I Am Makes a Difference', on my jacket above my heart. He gave me an extra ribbon and asked me to find somebody else to honor. As I was driving home tonight, I started thinking about whom I would honor with this ribbon, and I thought of you. I want to honor you.

"My days are really hectic; and when I come home, I don't pay a lot of attention to you. Sometimes I scream at you for not getting good enough grades in school and for your bedroom being a mess. But somehow tonight, I just wanted to sit here and, well, just let you know that you do make a difference to me. Besides your mother, you are the most important person in my life. You are a great kid, and I love you."

The startled boy started to sob and sob, and he couldn't stop crying. His whole body shook. He looked up at his father and said, through his tears, "I was planning on committing suicide tomorrow, Dad, because I didn't think you loved me. Now I don't need to."

Encouragement is oxygen to the soul!

3. Limit them.

God sent judgment on the house of Eli because he would not restrain his sons for the evil they were doing. (1 Samuel 3:13) God expects us to discipline our children and set limits for them.

A father said to his teenage daughter: "Be in by ten tonight." She said, "I am not a child!" The father said, "I know. That's why I want you in by ten."

The Houston Police Department recently came out with nine rules for raising delinquent children:

1. Give your child everything he wants.
2. When he picks up bad words, laugh at him.
3. Don't give him any spiritual training.
4. Avoid using the word "wrong."
5. Pick up everything he leaves lying around.
6. Let him read and watch what he wants.

7. Argue in the presence of your child.

8. Give him no chores.

9. Always take his side against neighbors, teachers, and the police. They are all just out to get him.

I believe many of the problems we face in America today could be solved if we just had more mean mothers. The following story explains.

The Meanest Mother in the World

We had the meanest mother in the whole world! While other kids ate candy for breakfast, we had to have cereal, eggs, and toast. When others had a Pepsi and a Twinkie for lunch, we had to eat sandwiches. And you can guess our mother fixed us dinner that was different from what other kids had, too.

Mother insisted on knowing where we were at all times. You'd think we were convicts in a prison. She had to know who our friends were and what we were doing with them. She insisted that if we said we would be gone for an hour, we would be gone for an hour or less.

We were ashamed to admit it, but she had the nerve to break the Child Labor Laws by making us work. We had to wash the dishes, make the beds, learn to cook, vacuum the floor, do laundry, and all sorts of cruel jobs. I think she would lie awake at night thinking of more things for us to do. She always insisted on us telling the truth, the whole truth, and nothing but the truth.

By the time we were teenagers, she would read our minds. Then life was really tough! Mother would not let our friends just honk when they drove up. They had to come up to the door, so she could meet them. While everyone else could date when they were twelve or thirteen, we had to wait until we were sixteen.

Because of our mother, we missed out on lots of things other kids experienced. None of us has ever been caught shoplifting, vandalizing others' property, or even arrested for any crime. It was all her fault. We never got drunk, took up smoking, stayed out all night, or a million other things other kids did. Sundays were reserved for church, and we never missed one service. We knew better than to ask to spend the night with a friend on Saturdays.

Now that we have left home, we are all God-fearing, educated, honest adults. We are doing our best to be parents just like Mom was. I think that's what is wrong with the world today. It just doesn't have enough mean moms anymore.

4. Lead them.

How do we lead our children? The words "parent" and "teacher" in the Hebrew language come from the same word. The answer is "monkey see, monkey do." You lead them by example.

Several years ago, I scolded my daughter Savannah for leaving her shoes on the floor in the living room rather than putting them in the closet. I will never forget what she said to me: "But, Daddy, you don't put your shoes in the closet." I said, "Savannah, you know you are right. Daddy should do this, and I'm going to start." Actions speak louder than words! Lead by example!

5. Laugh with them.

The Bible says, "A merry heart doeth good like a medicine . . ." (Proverbs 17:22). Children need to remember home as a place of joy and laughter. I encourage you to laugh and have fun with your children.

A little girl said to her mother, "Why do you have white hair mixed in with your black hair?" The mother said, "Every time you do something wrong, that makes me unhappy and it causes one of my hairs to turn white." The little girl then asked "How come all of grandma's are white?" Learn to laugh with your children!

6. Loaf with them.

Spend time with your children. Did you know a hundred years ago parents spent 54 percent of their waking hours with their children? Today we spend 18 percent of our waking hours with them. Parents are prone to give their children everything except the one thing they need most; and that is time – time for listening, time for helping, and time for guiding. It sounds simple; but in reality, it is the most difficult and most sacrificial task of parenthood.

James Boswell, the famous biographer of Samuel Johnson, referred often to a special day in his childhood when his father took him fishing. The day was fixed in his mind, and he often reflected upon many of the things his father had taught him in the course of their fishing experience together.

After having heard of that particular excursion so often, it occurred to someone much later to check the journal that Boswell's father kept to see what he had said about the fishing trip. Turning to that one date, the reader found only one sentence: "Gone fishing today with my son; a day wasted."

For the elder Boswell, it seemed to be a day wasted. For his son, it was a day which shaped him for the rest of his life. Fathers and mothers, I beg you to slow down and spend time with your children! It is more important than I can express.

A young, successful attorney said, "The greatest gift I ever received was a gift I got one Christmas when my Dad gave me a small box. Inside was a note saying, 'Son, this year I will give you 365 hours—an hour every day after dinner.'" My Dad not only kept his promise, but every year he renewed it. It is the greatest gift I ever had in my life. I am the result of his time."

7. **Lay hands on them.**

Jewish parents place their hands on their children and pray a blessing over them. The Scriptures they pray are: "The LORD bless thee, and keep thee: The LORD make his face shine upon thee, and be gracious unto thee: The LORD lift up his countenance upon thee, and give thee peace" (Numbers 6:24-26). The prayer they pray is actually threefold.

When they pray, "The LORD bless thee, and keep thee," they are praying for spiritual, physical, social, and mental growth of the child. Remember, these four areas are the ones in which the Christ child grew. (Luke 2:52)

Then they will ask for the Lord to make His face shine upon them. They are actually praying for God's presence in the child's life.

Lastly, they will ask for God to lift up His countenance. They are asking for God's approval and protection for the child.

You may be thinking: Is praying over my child really that important to God? In Hebrews 11, we have the Hall of Faith chapter that lists the great heroes of the Christian faith. Noah is there, and certainly he should be. He prepared an ark and saved the world. Moses is there; he led the children of Israel out of Egyptian bondage. Abraham is there; the Jewish nation began with him. But there are also a couple of other men in this Hall of Faith chapter: Isaac and Jacob. What did they do? They simply prayed blessings on their children. Yes, apparently praying for your children is so important to God that He even recorded it in the Hall of Faith chapter.

I remember when Savannah Abigail was dedicated to God. A dear friend of mine, Dr. Ed Ballew, preached the dedication message. I will never forget what he said to me from the pulpit: "Benny, don't you just pray *for* this girl. You pray *with* this girl." A regular practice of mine and her mother's is to pray blessing over her. I want to encourage every parent to take time to pray with your children. You don't have to know Greek or Hebrew or even the Bible cover to cover to talk to God about their needs.

I remember when Savannah was small and I would ask her if she had something she wanted me to pray about. She would many times request prayer for her dog Murphy, and we would pray for Murphy. The important thing is we prayed! I still ask her about the needs of her life, and we are still praying.

Allow me to share seven prayers for Savannah that you also can pray for your children. Pray that:

1. they will become "wise for salvation" early in life.
2. they will be protected from the enemy.
3. their "afflictions" will strengthen and teach them.
4. they will respect authority.
5. they will seek positive friends and avoid negative influences.
6. they will remain sexually pure.
7. they will submit to God in all things.

I also want to encourage you – even if your children are grown and away from home – to never quit praying for them.

A few years after I had been the pastor of Rock Springs Church, a precious saint of God, Fannie Freeman, started attending our church with her daughter-in-law. She was a precious lady in her eighties who loved God with all of her heart. Every Sunday, as she hugged my neck, she would whisper: "Pray for my son Marvin. I can't stand the thought of him dying without Christ and going to hell." This godly lady prayed for her son for more than fifty years. Finally, one Sunday morning, I saw him walk in the church and sit down by his wife and mother. When the invitation was given, guess who was the first one to the altar? It was Marvin! I assure you glory came down and Heaven filled our souls!

You can never convince me that God does not honor the prayers of a godly mother and father. Keep on praying and never give up! When it is the hardest to pray, pray the hardest. I assure you Marvin Freeman is grateful that his mother never gave up.

In 1993, workers doing some moving and remodeling at the Baseball Hall of Fame in Cooperstown, New York, discovered something rather unusual. As they were moving a display cabinet, they found an old photograph tucked behind the case. It was a photo of a stocky, friendly-looking man in a baseball uniform with the words "Sinclair Oil" on the shirt. Stapled to the picture was a note in a man's writing that said, "You were never too tired to play ball. On your days off, you helped build the little league field. You always came to watch me play. You were a Hall of Fame Dad. I wish I could share this moment with you."

No one knew how the picture got there or the identity of the dad in the photo. A national sports magazine picked up the touching story; and after publishing it, a man came forward to say he had been the one to tuck the photo and note behind the display case during a visit to the Hall of Fame.

It seems the ball player in the photo was his late father. Just like the note said, he was proud of his dad and believed he deserved to receive special recognition. So he decided to honor his father by holding his own little ceremony to induct his dad into the Hall of Fame.

That is wonderful! What this man was saying was: "Dad, you deserve a place alongside the best ball players ever. You were a Hall of Fame Father!"

I want to be a Hall of Fame Parent. Don't you? I trust and pray we will.

C H A P T E R   E L E V E N

Two small boys were having a conversation when one excitedly shared that he and his family had moved into a new house. He said, "It is wonderful! I have my own room; my brother has his own room; my sister has her own room; but my poor ole mom is still stuck in the room with Dad."

As sad as it is, in most cases, we must become parents before we can really appreciate our parents. I know I developed a new appreciation for my mother after sitting up many nights holding my own sick, little girl. I certainly began to realize the sacrifices she had to undergo because of her love and commitment to me and my sister. The following excerpt explains this point very well.

My Father When I Was ...

4 years old: "My daddy can do anything."

5 years old: "My daddy knows a whole lot."

6 years old: "My dad is smarter than your dad."

8 years old: "My dad doesn't know exactly everything."

10 years old: "In the olden days when my dad grew up, things were sure different."

12 years old: "Oh, well, naturally, Father doesn't know anything about that. He is too old to remember his childhood."

14 years old: "Don't pay any attention to my father. He is so old-fashioned!"

21 years old: "Him? My Lord, he's hopelessly out-of-date."

25 years old: "Dad knows a little bit about it, but then he should because he has been around so long."

30 years old: "Maybe we should ask Dad what he thinks. After all, he's had a lot of experience."

35 years old: "I'm not doing a single thing until I talk to Dad."

40 years old: "I wonder how Dad would have handled it. He was so wise and had a world of experience."

50 years old: "I'd give anything if Dad were here now, so I could talk this over with him. Too bad I didn't appreciate how smart he was. I could have learned a lot from him."

This reminds me of the story about the boy who at age sixteen said his father did not know anything and at age twenty-one thought his dad was pretty intelligent. The young man said he was amazed at what his dad had learned in only five years!

Four ways children can honor their parents are:

1. **Obedience.**

The Bible says, "Children, obey your parents in the name of the Lord: for this is right" (Ephesians 6:1). Why should children obey their parents?

Obeying is ethical in the eyes of God. When children disobey their parents, they must understand they are disobeying God.

One small boy said, "I have figured out how to get along with my momma. Whatever she says, I do it." Scores of children need to learn how to get along with their parents. An excellent place to start is with obedience.

Many times the problem is that children think they simply know more than their parents. I recently saw the following sign:

ATTENTION TEENAGERS: ARE YOU TIRED OF BEING HARASSED BY YOUR STUPID PARENTS? ACT NOW! MOVE OUT. GET A JOB. PAY YOUR OWN BILLS WHILE YOU STILL KNOW EVERYTHING!

Did you know there was once a child who knew more than his parents? We read about him in Luke 2:43-52. When Jesus was twelve, He and His parents went to Jerusalem for the yearly Passover Celebration that lasted seven days. After the celebration had ended, Joseph and Mary and the entire family left for home but Jesus stayed there. Joseph and Mary did not notice that Jesus was not with them for several days due to the large group traveling together. Can you imagine not being able to locate one of your children? Now just imagine losing God's own Son! I imagine Mary was fit to be tied! Three days later, they found Him in the Temple Courtyard. He was sitting among the teachers, listening to them and asking questions. His understanding and His answers stunned everyone who heard Him. Verse 48 says, "And when they saw him, they were amazed . . . ." You may appreciate what the word *astonishment* means: "to strike out, force out by a blow, but found only in the sense of knocking one out of his senses or self-possession; to strike with astonishment, terror, admiration." Verse 48 also says, "Son, why hast thou thus dealt with us? behold, thy father and I have sought thee sorrowing." Jesus said to His mother: "Why were you searching for Me? Didn't you know I would be in My Father's house?"

What is so amazing to me is verse 51. The Bible says "He returned with them to Nazareth and was obedient to them. The One who spoke the world into existence was obedient to His parents. The One who did not begin when the beginning began – He began the beginning! He obeyed Dad and Mom. Children today debate whether or not they should obey their parents!

Many parents are reading this and thinking this sounds great but also thinking: "How can I teach my child to be obedient?" The answer is discipline. The Bible says, "Foolishness is bound in the heart of a child; but the rod of correction shall drive it far from him" (Proverbs 22:15). We have thousands of cases of child abuse every year in America that never get reported. Let me share the circumstances of these cases with you.

It is when parents provide no discipline for their children. This is child abuse! We need to get back to the teachings of the Word of God and discipline our children. This is the answer for obedience.

2. Honor.

The Bible says, "Honour thy father and thy mother: that thy days may be long upon the land which the LORD thy God giveth thee" (Exodus 20:12).

Children usually go through four stages in their relationship with their parents:

1. They idolize them. ("My parents can do anything.")
2. They demonize them. ("Dad and Mom are the source of all my problems.")
3. They utilize them. ("Can I get the car Friday night?")
4. They humanize them. ("They are humans with a wealth of experience, and I can learn much from them.")

The Bible is very clear that parents are to be honored – no matter what. You may be thinking your dad and/or mom were never there for you, so why should they be honored. Well, think of it this way. If you walk into a court-room and see the judge behind the bench, would you refer to him by his first name? Absolutely not! He would be referred to as "Your Honor." The truth is that his character may be deplorable, but you still respect the position. We also should honor the positions of our father and our mother!

Allow me to share four practical ways to honor your parents:

1. Write them a note of appreciation. Do you realize you had nothing to do with your being born? Yes, 50 million sperm cells raced up a long canal; and one of them won the race, and you came into existence. Your parents gave you life! If you can't thank them for anything else, you can thank them for giving you life!

Talk show host Larry King reported that during his hospital stay he had many letters and gifts. King mentioned on his TV show the one that touched him the most was sent by Pete Maravich, former NBA star. Pete included a Bible and the following note: "Dear Larry, I'm so glad to hear that everything went well with your surgery. I want you to know that God was watching over you every minute; and even though I know you may question that, I also know that one day it will be revealed to you . . . because He lives."

One week later, King noted, Pete Maravich, college basketball and NBA luminary, died. Never underestimate the power of a note. Write one today!

2. Express appreciation for your parents to others. I encourage you to do this; and if possible, do it in the presence of others. This is a wonderful way to pay honor to them.

Three little boys were talking; and one of them said, "My dad is a lawyer. He can spend an hour in court and make $200." Another said, "That's noth-ing! My dad is a doctor, and he can spend an hour performing surgery and make $2,000." The other little boy said, "I have you both beat. My dad is a preacher. He can preach an hour on Sunday, and it takes eight men to take up the money!" Express to others appreciation for your parents.

3. Obey your parents completely and cheerfully. I see a lot of children obey their parents when they are asked to do something, but they do it with an "I really don't want to" look on their faces. Obey with style and with a smile!

4. Put your parents' interest before yours. A son walked into the kitchen on Mother's Day and saw his mother washing dishes. He became irate. He said, "Mother, today is your day. You get your hands out of that dish water! The dishes will still be there tomorrow." This is certainly not what I am speaking of! I am talking about doing something that will take the work off your parents. Cut off the TV, and go cut the grass. Get off the computer, and vacuum the carpet. Put down the phone, and pick up the furniture polish. By the way, if you are a boy and you think Dawn or Joy will wash off the macho, you may need a hormone shot.

The Bible says, "Let nothing be done through strife or vainglory; but in lowliness of mind let each esteem other better than themselves" (Philippians 2:3).

3. **Love.**

A first-grade boy came home from school and told his dad that his teacher had asked the class to write a report about the person they admired the most. He said, "Dad, I chose you." The dad could hardly hold back the tears until he asked his son why he had chosen him. The boy answered, "Because I couldn't spell Schwarzenegger."

The truth is that parenting is a difficult job, and children certainly owe their parents love. I recently read this letter exchange between a son and his mother.

The son left this message for her: "Washing the car – $5; taking out the garbage – $5. Total bill you owe me – $10."

The next meal the mother too had put a bill on his plate. It said, "Washing your clothes – $5; preparing your meal – $5; taking care of you when you are sick – $5; getting you to school on time – $5. Total bill – $0. I love you. Mom

Just as parents need to express love to children, children too need to express love to their parents.

Ways children can express love to parents:

A. By verbally expressing love. The Bible says, "Death and life are in the power of the tongue . . ." (Proverbs 18:21). I encourage every child (as long as there is one parent living, we are all still a child of someone) to let your parents know just how much they mean to you. I assure you no father or mother ever gets tired of hearing the words: "I love you."

Paul "Bear" Bryant, the legendary football coach of the Alabama Crimson Tide, was a one-of-a-kind type of guy. He was very hardnosed and disciplined, but he had a tender side. He made each of his players call home at least once a week and tell his mother he loved her. I remember, as a child, watching Coach Bryant on TV doing telephone commercials. In that gruff voice of his, he would ask, "Have you called your mama lately? I sure wish I could call mine." Call your parents and tell them "I love you" today.

B. By touching and embracing them. How long has it been since you gave your dad or mom a hug? See the truth about hugging below.

Hugging is healthy:
It helps the body's immune system;
It keeps you healthier;
It induces sleep;
It's invigorating;
It is rejuvenating;
It has no unpleasant side effects;
It is nothing less than a miracle drug!

Hugging is all natural:
It is organic,
Naturally sweet,
No pesticides,
No preservatives,
No artificial ingredients;
And it is 100 percent wholesome.

Hugging is practically perfect:
There are no moveable parts to break,
No batteries to wear out,
No periodic checkups,
Low-energy consumption,
High-energy yield,
Inflation proof,
Nonfattening,
No monthly payments,
Nonpolluting,
And, of course, fully returnable!

A man was trying to read a totally serious book, but his little boy kept interrupting him. He would lean against his knees and say, "Daddy, I love you." The father would give him a pat and say absently, "Yes, Son, I love you too"; and he would kind of give him a push away, so he could keep on reading. But this did not satisfy the boy; and finally, he ran to his father and said, "I love you, Daddy," and jumped up on his lap and threw his arms around him and gave him a big squeeze, explaining, "And I've just got to do something about it!"

C. **By keeping their commandments.** The Bible says, "If ye love me, keep my commandments" (John 14:15). How do we express love to our Heavenly Father? Simply by obeying Him. How do we express love to our parents? The same way, of course: by obeying them!

4. **Prayer.**

The last thing children owe their parents is prayer. One of the most touching times in my life occurred a few years ago when my doctor thought there was a possibility I had cancer. My emotions were wild the night before I was to go to the hospital for the final test. I remember Savannah coming up to me and saying, "Daddy, I know your test is going to be okay because I am praying for you." She then placed her little hands on me and asked God to take care of me. After that moment, I was ready to charge hell with a water pistol!

I know God heard her prayer, and that alone brought great comfort to my heart. By the way, there was no cancer! Pray for Dad and Mom. They need the prayer, and you need the practice!

CHAPTER TWELVE

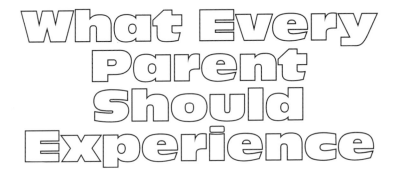

What Every Parent Should Experience

I will never forget Thursday evening, February 18, 1999. Barbara, Savannah, and I had been out for dinner and were driving home when Savannah, being five at the time, said, "Daddy, I would like to ask Christ into my heart." I said, "Savannah, that's wonderful! As soon as we get home, let's talk about it." Once we reached home, I went in and got busy doing a few things; and I will never forget what Savannah did. She came up to me and said, "Daddy, I thought we were going to talk about me accepting Jesus." I immediately apologized for my negligence, and Barbara and I sat down with her and began to explain to her the plan of salvation. Even now I cannot hold back the tears when I recall how she, with childlike faith, repeated the simple sinner's prayer with me.

We prayed just a brief prayer, and she asked Christ into her heart. Remember, it is not the length of the prayer but the strength of the prayer that makes the difference. I promise you what Barbara and I experienced that night was something that will forever be in our memories. My prayer for all parents is that they experience knowing that their children have accepted Christ. Possibly, they too could be there to guide them through this greatest choice of life.

Savannah was adopted; therefore, her mother and I were not there for her physical birth. I have often told her if I could have chosen to be at either the physical birth or the spiritual birth, I would have chosen the spiritual birth!

I think it is vitally important that children accept Christ at a young age. Did you know that after the age of twenty-five the odds are one in 10,000 for a person accepting Christ? After the age of thirty-five, the odds are one in 50,000; after age forty-five, it's one in 200,000; and after the age of sixty-five, it is one in 500,000! I believe that is why the Bible says, "Remember now thy Creator in the days of thy youth, while the evil days come not . . ." (Ecclesiastes 12:1).

Statistically, 85 percent of people who become Christians accept Jesus before the age of fourteen. Church, do we really believe this? Do we consider these statistics when we plan our yearly budgets? We need to!

I also would like to encourage adults not to discourage children from coming to Christ at a young age. Many times we think they must become older and have a crime-to-Christ testimony. But I think it is a far greater testimony when God saves someone from sin rather than in sin. A testimony is not how bad you were but rather how good God is.

I love Mark 10:13-16 when some parents brought their young children to Jesus so that He could touch them. Let's pick up the story at the end of verse 13:

"[And] his disciples rebuked those that brought them. But when Jesus saw it, he was much displeased, and said unto them, Suffer the little children to come unto me, and forbid them not: for of such is the kingdom of God. Verily I say unto you, Whosoever shall not receive the kingdom of God as a little child, he shall not enter therein. And he took them up in his arms, put his hands upon them, and blessed them."

You see, Jesus had just been dealing with the Pharisees over the very deep subject of divorce. So the disciples thought Jesus was too busy with the learned doctors of religion to be bothered with little children, but He kindly set them straight in a hurry!

Sometimes we think a little child has to become like an adult to understand the things of God, but Jesus says the adult has to become like a little child. Children can be and should be saved at an early age.

The great theologian and writer Matthew Henry, whose Bible commentary many of us still use today, was saved at the age of eleven. The great American preacher and theologian Jonathan Edwards, considered by many to be the greatest mind this nation has ever produced, was saved at the age of eight. Charles Haddon Spurgeon, "the prince of preachers," was saved when he was twelve. He later said he would have been saved earlier if there had been someone to instruct and guide him.

The Southern Baptist Convention recently revealed that 90 percent of their missionaries were converted before they were eleven years old. The average age for these conversions is eight. My hero in faith, Dr. John Maxwell, became a Christian at the age of three.

Parents, the greatest thing you can do for your children is to hand down your faith. I am convinced the way to do this is threefold:

1. **First is through a dedicated life.**

As parents, we must exemplify two things to our children. **The first step is a faith that is displayed.** I recently read that 89 percent of everything we learn is visual.

There was a young Jewish boy who once lived in Germany. His father was a successful merchant, and the family practiced the Jewish faith. But they moved to another German city, and the boy's father announced they would no longer attend the synagogue. Instead they would be going to the Lutheran church.

The boy was surprised and asked his father why the family was joining the Lutheran church. His father said for business reasons: "There are so many Lutherans in this town that I can make good business contacts at the Lutheran church."

The boy, who had deep interest in religion, became so disillusioned with his father's actions that something died within him. He said to himself: *My father has no real convictions.* The incident helped to turn him against religion with a vengeance. His name was Karl Marx, the father of communism. I wonder if Karl Marx would have turned out differently if he had seen genuine faith exemplified by his father?

I would like to say an encouraging word to single Christian parents. You can set a godly example for your child and see him or her follow the ways of God – even though your child's other parent is maybe not a Christian or a part of his or her life.

Notice what Paul said about his son in the Lord: "When I call to remembrance the unfeigned (sincere) faith that is in thee, which dwelt first in thy grandmother Lois, and thy mother Eunice; and I am persuaded that in thee also" (2 Timothy 1:5).

Timothy's dad was a pagan, unbelieving Greek; but he had a mother and a grandmother in whom he saw genuine faith, and he became one of the greatest men of God ever. Actions speak louder than words; therefore, we must have a faith that is displayed.

The Little Chap Who Follows Me

A careful man I want to be,
A little fellow follows me,
I do not dare to go astray,
For fear he'll go the self-same way.

I cannot once escape his eyes,
What e'er he sees me do, he tries,
Like me he says he's going to be,
That little chap who follows me.

I must remember as I go,
Through summer suns and winter snows,
I am building for the years to be
That little chap who follows me.

The second step is a faith that is developing. According to the Bible (2 Timothy 3:14-15), from the time Timothy was a small child his mother taught him the Scripture:

> 14. But continue thou in the things which thou hast learned and hast been assured of, knowing of whom thou hast learned *them*;

> 15. And that from a child thou hast known the holy scriptures, which are able to make thee wise unto salvation through faith which is in Christ Jesus.

I cannot encourage families enough to teach the Scriptures to their children at an early age. There is a much greater possibility of their coming to faith in Christ. Please do not feel intimidated. You do not have to know Greek and Hebrew to begin teaching your children the Word of God. Begin by reading them Bible stories out of a book written on their age level. Use objects and situations of everyday life to teach them Bible principles.

I recall one time after I had performed a baptismal service when a little girl in the church came to me and said, "Pastor, the next time you wash the peoples' hair, I want you to wash mine too." "Well, I was not washing their hair," I said to her. I then explained in terms she could understand what baptism is all about.

This reminds me of the story about a little girl who saw her first baptismal service. When she got home and was taking a bath, she was baptizing all of her dolls. Her mother walked by and heard her say, "I baptize you in the Name of the Father, the Son; and in the hole you go." I am simply saying use everyday events and objects to teach the Bible.

Did you know the Welch's grape juice company was formed to use the juice for communion? Do you know why pretzels are shaped in a figure eight? In 1610 A.D. the reward for diligent praying by Christian monks was pretzels. The monks prayed with their arms crossed in a figure eight. Did you know that restaurants have their origin in Scripture? The first restaurant was started in 1766 in France. Placed above the door was the Scripture: "Come unto me, all ye that labour and are heavy laden, and I will give you rest" (Matthew 11:28). Even the word *restaurant* comes from the word *rest*. Again, use the things around you to teach Bible principles to your family.

2. **Second is through a dependable life.**

Harvard University Research states four keys for a successful home: a dad that is strong in discipline, a mother that is available, affection that is in the home, and a family whose activities bring them together. Let's look more closely at these four areas:

A. A dad that is strong in discipline. You may say, "But my children don't need correcting. They are little angels." I know they are all little angels. But, let me tell you, as their legs get longer, you are going to find their wings get shorter. All children need discipline. Allow me to share six rules that will assist you in discipline:

1. Begin early. "He that spareth his rod hateth his son: but he that loveth him chasteneth him betimes" (Proverbs 13:24). *Betimes* literally means "early." Correction should begin when the child is old enough to knowingly and willingly disobey.

2. Let spanking be your last resort, not your first option. Jesus said, "As many as I love, I rebuke and chasten . . ." (Revelation 3:19). Try speaking before spanking.

3. Discipline promptly. Deliver the discipline as close to the time of disobedience as possible.

4. Father and mother need to present a united front in discipline. Do not let one do all the spanking and the other do all the hugging. As a matter of fact, one parent can hold the child while the other ministers the discipline. Then both can hug the child when it's over. Children are clever. They will play one parent against the other if allowed to do so.

5. If the decision is to spank, do a good job. If a spanking is warranted, do it in the right *place*, at the right *time*, and in the right *way*. The great thing about a good spanking is that if you do it right you won't have to do it real often. A few good spankings and your spanking days should be more or less over. You should not have to constantly swat at your kids.

6. Always discipline in love. Chastise your children; then sit down and cry with them, hug them, and let them know you love them.

B. A mother that is available. Mothers are so busy today working out of the home which can make the need for availability great all over our land. Mothers, may I say to you **the call to motherhood is a high calling**. If there is any possible way you can stay home with your children until they reach school age, do it! I assure you that you will never regret it. Remember, mothers are not keepers of the office but keepers of the home. (Titus 2:5)

I believe too many women are made to feel inferior for being mothers and housewives. Tony Campolo recently shared this story:

"When I was on the faculty of the University of Pennsylvania, there were gatherings from time to time to which faculty members brought their spouses.

— 123 —

Inevitably, some woman lawyer or sociologist would confront my wife with a question: 'And what is it that you do, my dear?' My wife, who is one of the most brilliant, articulate individuals I know, had a great response: 'I am socializing two homo sapiens in the dominant values of the Judeo-Christian tradition in order that they might be instruments for the transformation of the social order into the theologically prescribed utopia inherent in the eschaton.' When she followed that with: 'And what is it that you do?,' the other person's 'A lawyer' just wasn't that overpowering."

Granted, some mothers must work outside the home. If you are one who does, I want to implore you to be available for your family as much as possible.

C. Affection in the home. Dad and mom, let the children see you expressing love to each other and express love to them as well. When Mother Teresa received her Nobel Peace Prize in 1979, she was asked, "What can we do to promote world peace?" Her answer: "Go home and love your family."

D. Family activities. Families need to play together, eat together, relax together, and pray together. A survey was taken of 1500 children. They were asked: "What makes a happy family?" None of them replied, "Money, lots of toys, computer games, a big house, or cars." Instead the vast majority said, "Doing things together."

The Bible is never out of touch or out of date, and it speaks of four important times to spend with our children: "And thou shalt teach them diligently unto thy children, and shalt talk of them when thou sittest in thine house, and when thou walkest by the way, and when thou liest down, and when thou risest up" (Deuteronomy 6:7).

1. Mealtime: Families need to get back to eating together. Mealtime is simply a good time to slow down, be real, and connect.

2. Travel time: Moses spoke of teaching kids as we travel along the road. It is a great time to turn off the radio or TV and converse with your child.

3. Bedtime: Our most intimate conversations with Savannah happen at bedtime. For some reason, she is more vulnerable and transparent at bedtime than during the day. She is almost always ready to talk. (Of course, it could be a stall tactic.) Nevertheless, I have found it to be a great time to ask her about the needs in her life. After she shares them with me, we pray together.

Truett Cathy, founder of Chick-fil-A, shared the following story in his book *It's Easier to Succeed Than to Fail:*

My daughter Trudy, home from college for the weekend, told me as we were seated in the family room: "You know, Dad, the most favorable memories I have of you are the times when you came to my bedside and you let me tell you all the things I did during the day."

What? I asked myself. *I don't remember doing that very often.* I thought my daughter would remember our comfortable home, her fine education we provided, nice clothes, an automobile....

Instead, my daughter's fondest memories were of something that did not cost money. How I wished I could have turned back the clock. I would provide all the time my daughter wanted to share with me, especially at bedtime.

4. Morning time: Moses listed "rising up" as the final opportunity we have each day with our kids. A few of the things we try to do to assist Savannah in having a good day are that I pray blessing over her each morning and her mother wakes her with love and affection. Barbara even puts notes in her book bag. They are simply notes of love, encouragement, and motivation. By the way, Barbara also puts them in my suitcase when I am traveling.

The following story is a synopsis of what I am saying. It really spoke to my heart.

"Daddy, how much do you make an hour?" With a timid voice and idolizing eyes, the little boy greeted his father as he returned home from work.

Greatly surprised, the dad gave his son a glaring look and said, "You're too young to know that. Besides, I'm tired. Don't bother me now."

"But, Daddy, just tell me, please! How much do you make?" the boy insisted. The father finally gave up and replied, "Twenty dollars an hour."

"Okay, Daddy. Could you loan me ten dollars?" the boy asked. Showing his restlessness, the father yelled, "So that was the reason you asked how much I earn? Be still and go to sleep."

After it was dark, the father began reflecting on his impatience. He felt a bit guilty. Maybe, he thought, my son wants to buy something. To ease his mind, he went in to his son's room to see if he was still awake.

"Are you asleep?" he whispered.

"No," replied the boy, partially asleep. Then his dad gave him a twenty-dollar bill and said, "Here's the money you asked me to loan you earlier."

"Thanks, Daddy!" he smiled. "Now I have enough. Now I have twenty dollars." When his father looked confused, he looked at his son as if to say: "What do you want to buy?"

"Daddy, could you sell me one hour of your time?"

3. **Third is through a discerning love.**

In his book *Hide and Seek,* James Dobson researched 1,738 middle-classed boys and girls to determine high or low self-esteem and found the following qualities in all those with high self-esteem:

1. They were told they were loved and appreciated by their parents.

2. They had strict discipline.

3. They had open communication at home.

One little boy said, "The first two years of life, you are taught to walk and talk; and the next sixteen, you are told to sit down and shut up."

Let's get real practical. When is the time right to lead your child to Christ? Allow me to share three suggestions that may help you:

1. Pray for wisdom.

2. Be sensitive and notice the questions the child asks about God and the church.

3. Always be willing to openly express your faith to your child.

Once you feel the time is right, these are the steps I encourage you to follow:

1. **Explain why an individual must be saved.** Share that all have sinned (missed the mark) and come short of God's glory. (Romans 3:23) There must be payment for sin. The payment was paid in full by Jesus Christ. He paid the sin debt with His blood on the cross.

2. **Explain *how* to be saved.** I often tell people it is as easy as ABC:

A- Acknowledge your sins.
B- Believe Jesus died for your sins.
C- Confess your sins to Christ.

3. **Pray the sinner's prayer, and let your child repeat it with you.** Sample: "Lord, I am a sinner. But I am sorry for my sin – so sorry I want to change. I believe that You died for my sins, and I confess them to You. Thank You, Lord, for forgiving me and accepting me as Your child. Amen."

4. **Tell them why they are saved.** It is not on the basis of how they feel but on what the Word of God teaches. Feelings are fickle; but God is a fact, not a feeling. A person is saved if he or she accepts Christ because God said they were and because it is impossible for God to lie. (Titus 1:2)

5. Celebrate it in a big fashion. I remember after Savannah's salvation we went to Burger King and ate and played on the playground. We still celebrate her spiritual birth every February 18. It is a very big deal! The most important decision in her life!

6. Encourage your children to share their experience with others. Savannah called her grandmother (Nanny), teacher, and friends to tell them of her experience. The Bible teaches that salvation involves confessing to God and others. (Romans 10:9-10)

It has been my honor and privilege to lead many children to faith in Christ. All of them have been special, but none compare to leading my own daughter. Dad and Mom, you lead your children to Christ. You do not have to be ordained or be a Bible scholar to do this. Hand down your faith. It will be the greatest gift you will ever give!